"This is so much more than just a career book. This is the ultimate guide to owning your body, talents, and power as a woman."

Susan Hyatt, best-selling author of *Bare*, Master Certified Life & Business Coach, CEO, and founder of the University for Life Coach Training

"*Closing the Confidence Gap* addresses so many important issues impacting female professionals and gives them the tools to understand how to lead more by doing less, allowing them to maintain balance while still advancing their careers. These tools are crucial to helping women avoid the overwhelm and burnout that unfortunately have come to characterize our notion of success."

Catherine Hinckley, international government affairs, policy, and trade expert in the satellite industry, the pharmaceutical industry, and the White House

"When you're done reading *Closing the Confidence Gap*, you'll have a blueprint for believing in yourself, articulating your values, and recognizing your unique capabilities. You will come away with a strong belief in the real value you can provide across any type of organization. If you're at all stuck, confused, or mired in doubt and feeling unclear, this is the book for you!"

Tara Kristick, vice president and head of program management, Global Telecommunications Company

"This book is jam-packed with life-changing nuggets of information, including specific conversations to increase your salary and ask for what you deserve. If you're ready for a confidence booster so that you can lead the way in all areas of your life, then this is the book for you."

Angela Champ, human resources executive and author of *The Squiggly Line Career: How Changing Professions Can Advance a Career in Unexpected Ways*

AUTHOR'S NOTE

Throughout this book, the names of clients have been changed to protect their privacy. The personal stories in this book are written to the best of my memory, and I've consulted with individuals featured in or with knowledge of the stories to ensure they are written as best we can recall.

www.amplifypublishing.com

Closing the Confidence Gap: Boost Your Peace, Your Potential, and Your Paycheck

For more information, please contact:
Amplify, an imprint of Amplify Publishing Group
620 Herndon Parkway, Suite 320
Herndon, VA 20170
info@amplifypublishing.com

Library of Congress Control Number: 2022906888

CPSIA Code: PRV0522A

ISBN-13: 978-1-63755-420-3

Printed in the United States

To Hailey:
always remember who you are.
Love, Mom

CLOSING THE CONFIDENCE GAP

Boost Your Peace,
Your Potential,
and Your Paycheck

Kelli Thompson

amplify
an imprint of Amplify Publishing Group

CONTENTS

INTRODUCTION

Your playing small does not serve the world. There is nothing enlightened about shrinking so that other people will not feel insecure around you. We are all meant to shine, as children do. It is not just in some of us; it is in everyone, and as we let our light shine, we unconsciously give others permission to do the same. As we are liberated from our fear, our presence automatically liberates others.

MARIANNE WILLIAMSON

'd love for you to answer the following question:

What would you do if you had more confidence?

In preparation for this book, I've asked almost five hundred women this question. Here are some of their answers:

- Speak my truth and my ideas, without worrying what others think.
- Take more leading roles.
- Stand up for myself.
- Finally start my own business.

- Be fearless and stop second-guessing my abilities.
- Find a job that's a better fit for my talents.
- Ask for a raise.
- Run for office.

. . . and hundreds more answers that include women showing up, speaking up, taking up more space, and realizing their dreams.

I never set out to write a leadership book. In fact, I remember sitting in my boss's office one day, chitchatting about our dreams, and I mentioned to her that I'd always wanted to write a book. With absolute certainty, I stated, "I don't know what I want to write about, but I definitely know it won't be a leadership book. Ever." My logic at the time was that there were too many leadership books on the market, and I didn't want to compete with them. In my mind, I was thinking about books I'd read like *Good to Great* by Jim Collins, *7 Habits of Highly Effective People* by Stephen R. Covey, and *Execution* by Jack Welch. (Along with many others—all of which happened to be written by men.) We laughed and agreed that was definitely a category we didn't want to enter into and compete with.

I grew up in a small town and went to a Catholic school. Naturally, all the leaders (bishops, priests, etc.) were men. Women did not have a part in the church nor in the school leadership. Men were the principals and superintendents, while most teachers were women. In college, the deans and most of my professors were men.

After college, in 2002, I went into investments and banking, and it was not uncommon for me to be in rooms where I was one of the only women at the leadership table. I designed and developed leadership training programs that taught leaders how to give feedback, manage performance, hold crucial conversations, give recognition, and foster the skills the company deemed necessary to be a good leader or working professional.

While I worked at organizations that had wonderful benefits for working moms, like lactation rooms and flexible work in case I had to take my daughter to the doctor, the unconscious message was clear: I had great benefits, but I wasn't invited to lead beyond a certain rung of the ladder. My growth would be capped at some point because there were no women at the top. I shrugged it off, feeling helpless to change it. That was just the way it was.

Then, in 2019, everything changed. I left corporate America. As a new entrepreneur and coach, learning the dos and don'ts of being a business owner, I came across something in the entrepreneurship world that I'd never experienced in corporate America—masterminds. These were groups of women who met regularly, and the events typically consisted of business education, leadership skill development, networking, and community support. Coming into my first few meetings, I didn't know what to expect. I was just excited and hopeful to learn skills to make my new business successful.

In these group sessions, we talked about everything I didn't know I needed: doubt, imposter syndrome, speaking up and asking for what you deserve, money mindset and wealth gaps, women's health, work-life boundaries, and the challenges of relationships and parenthood as it related to career. We safely discussed what it felt like to be the only woman in the room, to be spoken over, and to have ideas dismissed. We shared our regrets of holding back in doubt and uncertainty, only to watch our male colleagues, qualified or not, confidently show up and assume roles we wanted.

For the first time in my life as a woman leader and professional, I felt seen and supported just being me. The spaces we met in were bright, welcoming, and fully stocked with coffee, healthy snacks, and even tampons right out in the open! (I had learned to be an expert tampon hider in my corporate office by sneaking it up my bra strap on the way to the restroom.) In the virtual spaces, we welcomed each other without a strict dress code. It didn't matter if you showed up with kids or no kids. We learned together, laughed together, and talked about solutions specific for women so we could feel empowered, trust ourselves, and create the businesses we wanted. We supported one another to be the leaders we wanted to be. I felt a mix of emotions a few weeks into my first mastermind meeting series. I felt seen by my group members and sad I didn't have this sooner. It felt like finding a piece of me that I didn't know was missing.

I thought to myself, this is exactly the missing piece I needed in corporate America.

I needed a group of women from across the country from various industries that I could learn from, with training and personal coaching to help push me to be my best. I would have had broader access to new ideas, pushed outside my comfort zone, and likely been more confident and effective. I would have had a safe place to talk about the real doubts I felt as a woman in the workplace and the challenges I faced as a working mom, and to learn strategies from other women to speak up and show up with more confidence. I needed a place where I could just show up as me, without having to hide vulnerability or doubt.

Men have this kind of support container by default because they are predominately in the decision-making rooms. Because most women didn't work outside the home during the rise of the modern organization, the work schedule, the buildings, the dominant leadership styles, and the training were all defined by men. I want to be clear that this is not men versus women. I've worked for wonderful male leaders, read their books, and am married to the best one on earth. This is about recognizing that the systems have been designed by one gender, and there is an opportunity to bring women together in a place where they feel seen, supported, and empowered to develop the skills they need to advance at work.

The sadness of realizing what I'd been missing in corporate America turned into a fire I couldn't smother. I scoured the internet looking for corporate women's leadership programs that brought women into a support container like this. I couldn't find anything like it designed with the topics I felt to be most important that I'd learned in my years of leadership development, personal coaching, and business ownership. I wanted to create relevant topics, such as owning your leadership style, discovering your unique talents, trusting yourself, boosting confidence, and amplifying your voice, that were made exclusively for corporate women. So I used my decades of training and leadership development and coaching expertise to create what I now call the Clarity & Confidence Women's Leadership Program, and I launched the first cohort in the fall of 2019.

I loved watching the transformations I saw women make in a few short weeks. They left with more confidence, feeling better in their own skin. They gained clarity on what they stood for as a leader. They found their voice and the courage to speak up more at work. They learned to stop second-guessing, trust themselves to make the right decisions, and not default to others' opinions. They took brave next steps to create a career they love. Plus they enjoyed being surrounded by a group of women inspiring them to lead at the next level. Many participants reflect that this is the first corporate leadership program they've experienced that addresses important skills women most struggle with in the workplace; it offers real solutions and a safe community to overcome problems with these skills so they can lead with clarity and confidence.

These experiences and transformations inspired me to do what I said I would never do: write a leadership book. This book you're holding in your hands is dedicated to helping women leaders advance with more clarity and confidence at work. A woman leader isn't someone who manages people; she's any woman who wields influence.

Unfortunately, doubt and imposter feelings are two big reasons I see women lack confidence, which holds them back from moving forward on their goals. But I suspected women didn't just bring these feelings upon themselves and that there were likely gender-workplace dynamics at play. This is because many of the men I worked with, and coached early on in my practice, didn't seem to struggle with confidence like women did. If they felt doubt, they didn't want to talk about it, and they hid it well while they anticipated their next opportunity, promoted their work, and took action.

THE CONFIDENCE GAP

Exuding more confidence can be a tricky game; at least that's what Judd Kessler, associate professor at Penn's Wharton Business School, found. For women, if you promote yourself too much or rate yourself too highly, then you might be seen as a bragger, egotistical, or full of yourself. If you never speak on your own behalf or underrate your value and performance, then it could signal a lack of confidence in your work. Kessler found that the way you view your work performance can vary depending on several factors, but the primary one is gender. His research found that women tended to outperform men on a standard test, but men felt more confident than women in their performance. In addition, men were more likely to self-promote their efforts, which in this study led to more job offers and higher starting salaries.

The bottom line, according to the research, was this: If you promote yourself more positively, it can have real benefits for you, but there is a gender confidence gap. The best recommendation the researchers gave was to start telling women they performed better than the men and hope their confidence would follow suit.

This isn't going to cut it. To close the confidence gap and see more women showing up in their full potential at work, we need more women leaders at the top of organizations. In far too many companies, there still aren't women in leadership positions. In 2021, women held just 6 percent of CEO positions in the United States, and only 24 percent of C-suite leaders are women. Women of color remain embarrassingly underrepresented at every level of leadership. Women also receive less leadership support than men at every level, with more men having access to leadership coaching and training opportunities.

A NEW APPROACH TO WOMEN'S
LEADERSHIP DEVELOPMENT

The leadership programs needed for the future of work must grow beyond a narrow set of skills that have permeated leadership training for decades, beginning at a time when leadership training was created for male leaders by male leaders. It's time to leave behind outdated leadership programs that shape women into old leadership styles and standards and then penalize them for using the same leadership qualities men do. Most corporate leadership programs today don't address the unique workplace challenges women face and how to succeed in spite of those challenges. I know this because I studied them, created them, and taught them for over a decade as a corporate leadership development and HR director. Instead, they focus on training leaders on strategy, processes, feedback, and company-specific policies—which are all important—and the best ones include some self-awareness tools. But many successful leaders say developing their intuitive and emotional intelligence, not a prescriptive leadership framework, is the key to their success.

Couple the doubt and imposter syndrome women feel with systemic issues, like the gender pay gap, the confidence gap, the leadership development gender gap, workload burnout, and systemic gender equity issues that plague women in the workplace today, it's no wonder that so many women experience this confidence gap, causing them to undervalue themselves and their abilities.

These doubtful thoughts and systemic issues are expensive—they cost women, and their organizations, in their peace, their potential, and in their paychecks.

To make real changes in the workplace, women need to see themselves in the rooms where decisions are made. They need to see women using healthy self-promotion and advocacy. By prioritizing women in leadership, companies can create bigger spaces where women feel seen, heard, and valued—and even more confident. Organizations need to address the systemic issues that keep women from showing up as their most clear and confident selves. This is not just an equality issue but an economic issue—when women lead, as research shows time and again, organizations are more successful and profitable.

As women, we need to do our part. It's time to own who you are, trust yourself, amplify your voice, and show up as the authentic, powerful woman leader you are meant to be. Your showing up frees other women to do the same. The world needs more women leaders, but this is not a "the future is all female" battle cry. We need *all* of us—men, women, and folks who identify in-between—to create a more inclusive, prosperous future.

As I developed and evolved my coaching and training practice for women, I made it my personal mission to help women advance to the rooms where decisions are made. That is why I wrote this book. There are systems that need to change, yes, and we are each one powerful woman inside a system that can impact the change we want to create. We can do this by investing in and inspiring just one woman at a time.

It's time to overcome doubt and close the confidence gap so women can accomplish their goals and make an impact in the rooms where decisions are made. Imagine the effects to women in the workplace if each one of us had less doubt and more confidence to act on what we want and who we are meant to be.

HOW TO USE THIS BOOK

The chapters in this book are my women's leadership program framework, which is built upon important data regarding women in the workplace today, the challenges they face, and tested leadership strategies they can use at work and home. Hundreds of my clients have used this approach to live and lead with more clarity and confidence in a way that feels authentic to them. You can download all the tools in this book to use in the moments that matter most to you.

This book will not teach you a specific set of rules to follow to be successful; we already have too many of those. In fact, as I share my stories, I've learned that following all the rules to success often leads us to the wrong place and showing up as who we think people want us to be, not as who we really are. This is exhausting and it kills our confidence. There are no three easy steps to showing up with more confidence.

This book won't teach you to play political games, provide you the latest tips to be more strategic, or give a prescriptive formula to be an ideal leader. This book will not teach you how to find more time to hustle to accomplish all the things to make you more successful or confident. In fact, it will show you how to lead more by doing less.

This book will teach you how to own who *you* are and use the talents for which you've been created. It will teach you how to live and lead with more confidence by leading from your values and trusting your gut. It will help you trust yourself and take your bravest next steps—so you can advance to the rooms where decisions are made and create a career you love. It will highlight the real and present issues that plague women in organizations today and how you can succeed despite these challenges. At the end of each chapter, it will invite you to notice opportunities for you to use the concepts discussed; own your unique approach or skills; if applicable, reframe your thinking; and provide a prompt to take action so you can boost your peace, your potential, and your paycheck.

This book will help you become the leader you are meant to be, not the one your organization wants you to be. Yet everyone still wins! Women learn to lead with more confidence, without losing themselves in the process, while their family, friends, and organizations benefit from their clear and confident leadership.

A clear and confident woman is a powerful woman. A happy woman. A woman who creates economic power for her family, her company, and her community. A confident woman changes policy. She creates a new way of living in the world, unapologetically, in tune with her own happiness. She inspires others to do the same.

I personally invite you to use this book to create the room you need to grow as a woman leader. Remember: you are a leader in any place you influence others. Whether you read it on an airplane, in your jammies in bed, or in a book club at work, I congratulate you on investing in yourself and your future. You have permission to shine. It's time to start a ripple effect.

Let's advance with confidence.

An Open Letter to CEOs and Executive Leaders:

While the content in this book is meant to support women in their everyday feelings of doubt and boost their confidence, remember that some causes of imposter syndrome—the feeling of being found out, discovered as unqualified—and a lack of psychological safety are systemic. Research shows that people experience greater imposter feelings when they work in fields predominantly filled by one gender, have experienced racial discrimination, or have seen that brilliance is prized above all else. Many underrepresented groups feel greater imposter feelings when they haven't seen themselves represented at the top.

While it's tempting to want to "fix" someone's confidence, let's also make sure that work environments are psychologically safe places to share ideas. A great place to start is to ask women at all stages in their careers if they feel that their ideas are welcome in meetings and contributions fully heard. Let's expand our definitions of "executive presence," which have typically been confined to a limited scope of masculine behaviors or expectations on how women "should" behave.

Let's be sure that executive leadership teams are places where everyone can see themselves no matter their gender, race, or ability. This is not about having one person of color or a woman, but making a commitment to have an executive team that reflects the diversity of your customer base. This is not just a social justice issue. Organizations with diverse executive teams recognize a 50 percent increase in profit. This is an economic issue that can't be ignored.

Closing the confidence gap is a both/and approach. It requires organizations to address the systemic issues that can impact a woman's confidence at work, *and* I wholeheartedly believe in supporting women in navigating the very real feelings of doubt and imposter syndrome. Let's change the system while also providing women the tools they need to advance with confidence.

1

CLAIM YOUR ROLE AS A CONFIDENT LEADER

To stand strong in what you feel and know, to me, that's the greatest bravery. That's true confidence, which means loyalty to self. Regardless of what others are calling "brave" at the moment: You stay loyal to yourself.

GLENNON DOYLE

I followed all the rules.

Both at work and home, most of my twenties and early thirties were spent listing and striving for all the things I was told would make me happy. I had a long list of shoulds, built from media portrayals of women, my family's expectations, my own expectations based heavily on my Midwestern small-town Catholic upbringing, and what I thought I'd need to be successful. I delighted in setting goals and feeling the tingles of excitement when I could check the box as accomplished.

My box-checking list included items like these:

- Graduate college in four years.
- Get married before the "good ones" are taken.
- Buy a house. Then a bigger one.
- Drive a nice car.
- Get a good job at a stable company with benefits.
- Work extra hard to get promoted.
- Have a baby young so you have plenty of energy. Also, your clock is ticking.
- Get a graduate degree—it's a family standard.
- Make six figures so you don't struggle for money.
- Keep your weight in check—preferably a size eight or slimmer.

I checked off items like a boss. For years it seemed to work well for me. I'd accomplished many things on my list, including finding roles in financial services firms that paid well and had great upward mobility. I married at twenty-three and had my daughter just two months shy of my twenty-fifth birthday. I used my employer's tuition reimbursement policy to fund my MBA degree and felt an extra sense of pride when I was invited to come back and teach as an adjunct management professor. My career was accelerating, and when new opportunities were presented to me at work, I took them. I felt flattered to be wanted, and the extra money and title boost didn't hurt either. While my career trajectory was nice and linear into my early thirties, I did find myself getting bored quickly, but the money was keeping my family afloat, so I kept on going. I needed to keep up my high salary as the breadwinner, especially when I filed for divorce from my first husband in 2011 and found myself supporting my daughter and me on my income alone. Showing that I could succeed as a single mom became another item to add to my list with a box to check.

I kept on pushing ahead in my life and career despite the shame I felt inside from the divorce; the messages I'd been taught for years in Catholic school said that divorce was a grave sin. The recurring thought of breaking this rule left my stomach fiery with guilt and brokenness. I felt like a failure, like I wasn't even smart enough to make my marriage work.

I rushed into my next relationship, made a career change, and turned my diet and fitness habits from healthy to obsessive, trying to regain a sense of happiness and belonging by adding more boxes and checking them. I tried my best to keep up with my daughter's interests and hobbies while I stretched my budget to take her on birthday trips instead of purchasing gifts, in hope she would remember the experience. Working to outhustle the guilt of the divorce, my talk track became *If I can just do the right things to be seen as a good partner, have a perfect body, be a good role model for my daughter and a competent leader, then I'll be happy. Everything will fall into place.*

All my box checking and rule following came to a head one morning, a couple of weeks after ending a long-term relationship with someone I thought I'd spend the rest of my life with. I pulled my coffee cup from the brewer and slumped into my kitchen chair. I picked up my pen to journal, but it felt heavy and useless. I hadn't slept well. There were so many thoughts fighting for space in my brain that none of them could win their way out onto the paper. All I could muster were tears, and I tried to hold them back as best I could because I didn't want red, puffy eyes coming with me to the office for the rest of the day.

So there I was with my coffee, and tears started flowing. I ruminated on the thought, *How the hell did you get here? If you're so smart, how did you make such poor choices, especially in your relationships?* I tried to stifle my ugly, snotty cries, but it wasn't happening. As someone who prided herself on being able to always hold her composure, I gave myself permission to do something I'd never done before, to just experience how awful and chest-crushing this all felt. And sob. I emailed my boss and told him that I wasn't going to be in until noon. I knew I wouldn't be able to pull myself together any moment soon, and tears at the office weren't exactly fashionable.

A kitchen-table meltdown ensued as I felt the weight of all my rule following and box checking come crashing down. One by one I reflected—and cursed—on how all this well-intentioned rule following left me in such a mess. It started when I ignored the doubts in my gut when I was walking down the aisle to marry my first husband. This evolved into my divorce from him seven years later, in which I kept half the debt from our relationship. I kept the house, which I couldn't afford, but stayed put not only because I wanted my daughter to keep some consistency but also because we purchased it at the top of the housing boom and still hadn't recouped what was paid. As a single mom with a divorce agreement that did not include child support, I was living paycheck to paycheck, with a credit card to fill in the gaps. At that moment I had nearly $40,000 in credit card debt alone, not including my house, car, and student loan payments. I spent too much money trying to keep up with my list of shoulds and working to provide my daughter and me a lifestyle I couldn't afford.

I wasn't in the mood to hurry into work that day because the ideal job that I'd transitioned into the year prior was unraveling.

I'd been hired to lead the human resources function of a technology company, and I loved it, but nine months into the role, we were acquired by a much larger publicly traded organization. I was given a new role focused on client education and marketing, but I wasn't as jazzed about it. While the team was fantastic, it just didn't give me the same amount of energy and use my talents like human resources and talent development work did. I found myself eyeing job posting boards again, wondering whether I was in the right career.

And to top it all off, I may have appeared like I was in great physical shape in my size two pants, but the diet industry had lied to me. I had never felt so miserable, food phobic, and self-conscious. So there I was, on the other end of two failed relationships, in debt up to my eyeballs, in my lying size two pants, wondering if I would ever love my career and trying to keep my act together to be a good role model for my daughter. My stomach burned with regrets. *Why did I make some of these choices? Why is this happening to me? How in the heck did I get myself here? How will I ever get myself out of this? I followed all the freaking rules!*

During my kitchen-table meltdown, I learned a strangely liberating truth: I was a hot mess, and it was my fault. There was so much going wrong here, and I could blame so many people and circumstances; however, there was a common denominator in all of this.

Me.

If there was good news, it was that if I could figure out how I got myself into this mess, I could also chart my path out of it. But that was going to make me vulnerable because it meant I first had to have the courage to look inside and recount all the wrong choices I made, boxes I checked without asking why, and red flags I ignored that led me to this moment. And then I felt a still, small voice whisper, *I have forgiven you, but you have not forgiven yourself.*

I mean, of course I had never thought to forgive or feel compassion for myself, especially for the divorce. That was something I did for other people but not myself. Those words felt so peaceful, so I embraced them and just sat still with my now-cold coffee. I wrote the whisper down in my journal and composed myself enough to head off to shower. I eventually made it into the office for a few hours that day and did my best to hide in my office with my puffy eyes, when I should have just given myself permission to rest and stay home.

FROM CHAOS TO CLARITY

The next few days and weeks, if I'm being honest, felt like crap. One of the concepts I learned from Harvard-trained sociologist Martha Beck in my life coach training is that real change doesn't feel good, because our whole life falls apart. Everything we thought we were, how we identify ourselves, dies and falls away. We're "back in square one" she says—and that's what it felt like. It's totally starting over, like a caterpillar that fully dies in its cocoon and turns into this soupy brown substance.

I call it *poop soup*.

In the aftermath of my kitchen-table meltdown, I felt like poop soup sloshing through the world, trying to figure out who I really was and what I really wanted. I was in liminal space, that place where nothing in my old life seemed to fit, but my future wasn't here yet, nor did I know what it would look like. I was terrified I would repeat old mistakes. I had bought into so many ideals of things I thought I needed, but I never stopped to ask myself if they were something I truly, deeply desired or if they were my culture's way of keeping me conforming to what was expected of me. My confidence was a roller coaster because I was hustling to keep up with what I thought people would approve of—it didn't bring me long-term happiness or confidence, just exhaustion and doubt.

I was totally bought into the mindset of *I'll do _____ by _____*, which simply set me up for failure. It also kept me believing the big lie of *I'll be happy when _____*. I hope I'm not raining on your happy parade, but there is no "happy when." I was just as miserable trying to keep myself a size two as I was when I was twenty pounds over my ideal weight—despite what the diet industry led me to believe. I was just as unhappy three months post–title and salary promotion as I was before I applied.

My poop soup phase moved at a snail's pace of trying to figure out how to have real compassion and self-forgiveness while also figuring out what I truly wanted. After a couple of months had passed, a meme from the new musical *Hamilton* was blowing up on social media. Alexander Hamilton asks Aaron Burr:

"If you stand for nothing, what will you fall for?"

Oh. My. God. That line sent shivers from my hips, up my spine, and into my brain. Mind blown. *How do I figure out what I stand for? How is it that I've never been intentional about claiming and explaining what I stand for? What have I fallen for because I've just defaulted to what I thought would be good for me? How do I do this now? Can I go back and change it all?* Well, we know we can't do that, but I clung to some words from author and artist Teri St. Cloud. She says, "You can't go back and make the details pretty, but you can move forward and make the whole beautiful."

Deep in my poop soup phase, when I was coming to grips with the fact that I thought I stood confidently as a "strong woman," I was also allowing it to mean that I could tolerate a bunch of crap. Being a strong woman doesn't mean you have to settle for poor behavior or less than you deserve; being a strong woman means knowing exactly what you stand for and not allowing anything less. But I didn't know how to put language to that and make it a way of living and leading. As usual, the universe is just in time because the following Sunday, as I took my weekly walk around the trail near my home, my headphones played the book *Rising Strong* by Brené Brown. She says, "How can we expect people to put value on our work when we don't value ourselves enough to set and hold uncomfortable boundaries?"

As I paced down the trail and looked up at the trees, I asked myself, "Do I even know what my values are?" I started to beat myself up more than the one-hundred-degree heat on my shoulders. I mean, duh—how could I value myself if I don't even know what I value? Just like Hamilton rapped in the musical: because I didn't know what I stood for (my values), I was falling for everything. I was working harder on others' definition of *success* over my own. Claiming and naming my values would give me the language I needed to articulate what I stood for.

It was time to claim my role as a confident leader—in my life and my work.

THE ART AND SCIENCE OF VALUES

Turns out, **claiming and writing about your values is one of the most effective psychological interventions ever studied,** according to Kelly McGonigal, a Stanford psychologist, best-selling author, and TED speaker. She says that just ten minutes per day of writing about your personal values and intentions and how your day aligns with them produces confidence, health, and resilience-boosting effects months, and even years, later.

It's so easy to get caught up in checking all the boxes and agreeing to what looks good on paper. We forget that trusting our gut and following our heart have merit and fuel our confidence when they are in alignment. If we want to get clear on what we truly want, feel more confident, and stop exhausting ourselves to conform to others' standards, values become the bedrock in guiding the choices toward what you do and *how* you do it.

As a leader, leading by your values extends beyond the title you earned and guides *how* you are going to lead by defining how you will show up to your team. Will you be the woman who leads with hustle and overachievement or with empathy and balance? Who do you want to be described as? Articulating your values is about getting clear on what we truly want. When we do, we stop exhausting ourselves in conforming to others' expectations. Values become a guide not only for what choices to make but also how we execute those choices.

Stephen Hayes, a professor of psychology at the University of Nevada and one of the pioneers of acceptance and commitment therapy, reveals in his book *The Liberated Mind* that values are different than goals. He defines *values* as chosen qualities of being and doing; they are enduring, ongoing guides to living. While *goals* are finite, things we check off a list, values are the guide on *how* we achieve those goals. Goals often take us down the road of box checking, and if you are a high-achieving, focused person, it can be easy to keep your eyes on the goal without stopping and checking in with yourself: *Do I even want this? Is this aligned with my values and intentions? Is this what I truly want? Or am I trying to "win"?*

As I personally worked to get clear on my naming my values, I printed off a long list of values words I found in an online search. It seemed like many of the words could fit; thus, finding that clarity in knowing what I stood for and what I wanted felt overwhelming. Hayes recommends we narrow our values to three to five words. For me, in that moment, it felt easier to know what I *didn't want or value,* so I made that list.

Did not want list:

- People with poor anger management, emotional intelligence.
- Work that required too many layers of approvals.
- Debt and poor money choices.
- People unwilling to show up on time, make commitments, carry out promises.
- A company with all-male leadership.
- A "this is how we've always done it" mindset.
- Unwillingness to invest in personal education and self-development.

I reflected back on my list of "don't wants" and had an aha: What if the things I valued were the opposite of what made me angry on that list? What if the anger of a boundary being crossed was a sign that a core value was violated for me? For example, if it infuriated me to have to get six layers of approvals before a decision could be made, did it violate my value of creativity? Personally, what needs did I have in my relationships and at work that were a nonnegotiable and strained the relationship when they were missing?

This layer of clarity, eliminating what I don't want, helped me write a long list of what I wanted in my future relationships, financial health, family, and well-being. I wrote the answers to questions like: *What do I absolutely need from my relationships? What are my nonnegotiables for how I want to live my life with my daughter? Also, what do I need from my work?* I thought about why my previous employers, while great organizations, didn't feel fulfilling—*what was missing? What did I value in leadership?* I started to recognize that these values not only were going to be important for my personal life but could also have lasting implications on how I worked and in my leadership. I ended up with five values that rose to the top:

Love: To me, it means a sense of unconditional acceptance that doesn't depend on appearance, income, or work. It's seeing and accepting someone's humanity. Ultimately, it's self-love. We can only love others as much as we love ourselves.

Respect: For me, these are the little things, like showing up on time, the words people choose when they talk about others, treating and including all people, genders, and races with dignity. The words people choose often reveal the condition of their heart—revealing their level of respect.

Family: Family is about investing in your family and putting it first, but it also means having a career and family rhythm. This extends into work in the sense that I wanted to create a working environment that felt intimate like home—you feel seen, heard, and trusted.

Creativity: I need the space and authority to try new approaches to my work and develop brand-new programs or products, without the requirement of going through five layers of approvals.

Learning: I love learning for learning's sake and know that I am at my happiest when I'm learning something new. I realized I need an employer who valued offering learning opportunities. As an entrepreneur, I set aside a development budget for myself.

In the weeks and months after the messiness of that morning, clarity began to emerge by way of naming my values and leading my life in alignment with them. I committed to claiming my role as a clear and confident leader and living the next year of my life from my own values: with love, with respect, a focus on my family, bringing in creativity and learning. As I had new goals pop into my head, instead of blindly following them, I learned to first ask myself, *Is this in alignment with my values?*

I immediately thought about how I would put these values into action, and I started with the small things. I wrote down what my values look like in day-in, day-out reality. I wanted to be very clear on what these values meant to me and exactly how I perceived them showing up in words, decisions, and behaviors—both mine and others. I immediately felt a boost of confidence. Suddenly it felt conscious and intentional to lead my life forward in a way that felt true to me, not who my culture said I should be. Claiming my values felt empowering when I could begin to put my stake in the ground, but it also meant I had to give a hard no to everything that didn't align with them.

I evaluated my social media feed and unfollowed accounts or people that didn't align with these values. I noticed leaders who seemed to share the same leadership values as me and took notes. I realigned my financial habits, spending and saving in alignment with my values. I ended relationships that didn't align with my values. I took intentional action to create things in my life that aligned with my values by scheduling trips to see my family who lived out of state, enrolling in writing courses to satisfy my learning and creativity, and mainly focusing on loving myself first. After all, how could I be the best partner, mom, leader, or employee if I was looking to everyone else to make me feel loved? I was finally learning how to have some self-compassion and that loving myself first—even the parts that felt unlovable—was my responsibility.

Here's a tip to make your values actionable: make them an adverb. The simple trick here is to add a "with" before or an "ly" to the end of your values words and make them actionable. For example, when I had to have difficult conversations that included saying no or setting a boundary because it didn't align with my values, I focused on how I could hold those conversations respectfully and lovingly.

In my business, when things don't happen as planned, it's easy to get frustrated and get down on myself. To get out of my funk and back into right action, I'll often stop myself and ask, *How can I approach this with a learning mindset? How can I overcome this with creativity?*

LIVE AND LEAD WITH YOUR BEST YES

I've been there. My clients have been there. Climbing the ladder of success, only to get to the top to find that it's not only leaning against the wrong wall but perhaps against the wrong building. When you find this out, it sucks. It's not just a "Oh, good to know. I'll climb back down and switch buildings and climb back up." Finding that I was climbing the wrong building felt awful because I questioned everything I thought I knew and who I thought I was. Not only did it lead to my kitchen-table meltdown but it also took months to find a clear path forward. I had so much of my identity wrapped up in checking my boxes and in my relationship status, fitness level, titles, and work. So coming to grips with the reality that morning at the kitchen table that my ladder was against the wrong building caused a painful untangling of my *do* from my *who*. What I *do* is not *who I am*. I questioned my goals, my talents, and my worth. It felt disorienting.

It felt like poop soup.

So what do you do if you find yourself like I did, as the common denominator of too many failed relationships, projects, or roles that don't fit? That might be why you picked up this book—you know something isn't working or fitting. You may be leveling up at work, but it seems your confidence isn't advancing with you. Something feels off, whether it be your work, your leadership style, your relationship, or your well-being. First, have a ton of compassion for yourself. From the day we are born, women are launched into social conditioning about what we should want, how we should behave, and when we should accomplish certain things in our lives.

While your culture of upbringing may vary, most cultures are patriarchal, and they have norms by which women are expected to conform—whether personality, relationship, appearance, or occupational norms. They often tell women that being nice and tolerating poor behavior with a smile are more socially acceptable than directly telling people no and being assertive about what you want. I had to make peace with the messages I'd been taught growing up about what was expected of me and how I should act as woman leader, and instead ask myself what I truly wanted based on *my* values.

If you're rolling your eyes a bit with all this values talk, you're not alone. If I'm being honest, sometimes my clients gloss over or procrastinate when I assign my nonnegotiable homework for them to claim their values. I don't blame them, because I felt this way at one point too. Values have been worn out by being plastered on corporate web pages as a virtue signal but optionally being followed through on. So why bother? If you've been around the block of personal development, you may have done some values work. We're going to get clear on your career and leadership values and make them actionable—specifically to help you make clear and confident decisions.

In your life, and especially as a woman in the workplace today who will make and influence many decisions, so many things will look right. Knowing your values gives you the discernment—not between right and wrong but between what *looks* right and what *is* right. There will be so much ambiguity, so many competing goals, so much people conflict. There will be competing schedule demands and critical budgeting and spending decisions. There are many colleagues to poll and bosses who have opinions on the right thing for your career. People are eager to give you advice on the best decision you should make, and it's tempting to go along with popular opinion. There are just so many yeses and noes in a day. Your values inform you as to how you'll show up and take action in executing that choice.

> Knowing your values helps you choose **your best yeses and noes,** no matter what's popular, culturally appealing, or demanded of you.

Susan David, psychologist and author of *Emotional Agility*, sums this up best when she reminds us, "Values are the heartbeat of our why."

VALUES CREATE YOUR FOUNDATION AS A LEADER

While it was a personal turn of events for me that caused me to claim my values and get clear on what I stood for, it had a ripple effect into the way I worked and led. Without claiming my values, I wouldn't have had the guidance system I needed to make the decision to leave corporate, identify my ideal business model, and make the right client and financial decisions. It's important for women in leadership to have the courage to live by their values to define the way they work, choose, and lead.

Otherwise, we end up just copying someone else's style and hoping for good results.

My client Ellen was a well-known top performer at her technology firm. She'd been with the organization for years and developed a reputation as someone who could get things done and negotiate any tricky situation with a client, even though she wasn't in a client-facing role. When high-profile projects came down from leadership, they went to Ellen's team. Ellen was consistently promoted to manage the same people she once called peers. This was where things got tricky. Wanting to maintain her top-performer image, she said yes to nearly everything. She didn't want to disappoint her colleagues, and definitely not the owners of the organization. When she had to give feedback to her team, it just felt awkward because they used to be her direct coworkers.

When Ellen and I started our coaching, her goals were to set herself apart as a leader, be more discerning about the projects she took on, and have the skills to launch a new company initiative she'd just landed. We started where I start with all my clients, identifying and naming her values, which were empathy, innovation, excellence, balance, and family.

When she continued to get requests to sit in on client escalations, even though it wasn't part of her role, she'd recall her values of innovation and empathy—she let the requester know, empathetically, that she appreciated their ask, but that she'd need to decline so she could deliver on the innovative new project she'd been assigned.

When it came to her daily leadership, she wanted to be seen as someone who treated her team like family while also communicating her standards for excellence—also with empathy! She made a list of what actions and words it took to lead with excellence and considered other "excellent" leaders she admired. How did they lead meetings? Hold tough conversations? Set boundaries? She committed to trying the new approach and blended those qualities into her value system. Having a set of standards that guided what she said yes to, how she led her team, and what behaviors mattered to her as a leader helped her move forward with confidence.

Several months into our program, she said, "I feel like I've finally defined my leadership style, and because I have more balance from not saying yes all the time, I have more free nights at home with my family." When life gets crazy with major decisions to make, leadership actions to take, a team to lead, boundaries to set, or unplanned changes, coming back to your core values as a leader serves to keep you grounded yet it helps you make the next right choice for your family, your work, and your future.

Another one of my clients, Brandy, called me because she was super unhappy in her career. After lots of organizational changes that impacted her job, she felt frustrated, unseen, and underutilized at work. Her first homework assignment was revealing her values, which she determined to be stability, connection, authenticity, health, and family. She journaled on exactly how these values showed up in her home life and work life, and how these values would be apparent in the workplace. She wrote these values at the top of her notebook, and as she went on job interviews, she kept them front and center. She asked her interviewers questions that would help her determine if they made decisions aligned with those values—if the work she would actually be doing would be in alignment with her values.

This was critical to her success in finding a role she loved. She went on many interviews and turned down opportunities that wouldn't allow her to show up authentically or use her real talents. She passed on roles in which she didn't feel a connection to the people or the company's purpose. She ultimately chose a company that not only allowed her to bring her best talents to work every day but was well known for their commitment to employee health and flexible work to support working parents. She found a place where she felt safe to be a confident leader. Now, if she would have set a goal to have a new job in three months, she would have been disappointed and discouraged—or she would have maybe accepted the first offer that came her way to meet this goal, only to be miserable in her new job soon after hire because it was a poor fit.

When we force it, it fails us, doesn't it?

Launching her career search in alignment with her values allowed her to stay flexible on her timeline while finding a role she loved and was in complete alignment with the career she was working to create. How did she stay sane in her previous role while pursuing her career search? By setting energetic boundaries defined by her values. Even though her work environment was toxic, she focused on her own health—both mental and physical. She focused on the value of having stability in a paycheck while she looked for a new role. She focused on keeping her support network of personal connections close while she managed the transition.

Today, when I have to make decisions about my business, setting goals is important to keep the business afloat, but my goals can't come at the expense of my values. I first define how my business fits my core values, and then I create goals that align with that. For example, family is one of my values, and to me that means being home to spend quality time with them. So setting a goal of booking twelve speaking engagements per year could create a misalignment with my family value. Why? Because that would require more travel than I enjoy. But the good news about values, unlike goals, is they allow flexibility. When I look again at my goal of speaking engagements through my value lens of family, I can create a "while also" scenario. How can I achieve my goal of twelve speaking engagements *while also* honoring my family? Well, I can say yes to four in-person speaking events and book eight virtual events. This flexible approach leads to more clear, confident decisions that are effective and still aligned with the way I want to work.

At the end of the day, you are always teaching people how to treat you, whether it's your partner, your kids, your team, or your colleagues. Fall for everything, or promote yourself as a "tolerator," and people learn they can talk down to you, treat you as a pushover, or take advantage of your generosity. And you'll keep attracting that into your life. When you stand firm on your values and clearly claim your confidence that you are worthy of nothing less than love and respect—or your unique values—you are teaching people to treat you with such. Those who are looking for someone to push around will no longer be interested. It's okay to let them be angry about that.

Values-based leadership is critical for women because the system of work hasn't been designed for us; it was designed for men, by men, when women stayed home. So it can be easy to unconsciously fall in line with copying a leadership style that may not truly align with our unique style. It can be tempting to climb up the ladder, enjoying the money and accolades, without ever stopping to ask if it's leaning against the right wall. It can be seen as normal to conform to a culture of hustling and overworking, never putting a stake in the ground to demand a better, more human way of working. It's no wonder women are feeling more frustrated, exhausted, and burned out than ever before.

What I know is that when I'm clear on what I stand for, I gain clarity on the right choices and the right next steps. When I have the courage to communicate the stand I take personally and professionally, it's not always easy, and some don't like it. But the best thing is, when you stand firm in your values, and you find the people or organization who matches them, they're totally worth falling for.

HOW TO FIND YOUR VALUES

Values are not shoulds. When you make a list of values to help guide you toward the life you want to create, it can be tempting to create yet another list of shoulds. When I work with my clients on this exercise, it's inevitable that their first list of values is their shoulds. My parent says I "should" value empathy. My community says my top value "should" be faith. My network says my value "should" be achievement.

Another way values can be skewed is people listing what they perceive to be their strengths. While identifying your strengths is important, and we'll talk about that more in another chapter, your values will guide you toward *how* you use your strengths. Ultimately, values serve as a true north—while you never reach it, they will always guide you toward your next right step.

One way to discern whether something is a value for you is to notice how your body responds to the word. If you read the word *empathy* and your body tightens up and feels heavy or anxious (because Momma told you that kindness is king!), this is not a value for you. If you read the word *clarity* and your shoulders drop, your chest rises, and you feel free, that's likely a value for you. Your body is trustworthy here; she will not lie to you.

Values provide you clarity, not certainty. (Dang it!) Only our ego wants certainty, so when you can ask yourself, "Is this decision in alignment with my values?" or, "What would be the next right choice in alignment with my values?" You'll have more clarity on your right next step even when everything feels foggy. You can feel confident in claiming the roles you desire in work and life because you know they are genuinely and honestly in alignment with your truest self.

CLOSE THE CONFIDENCE GAP TOOL KIT

CLAIM YOUR ROLE AS A CONFIDENT LEADER

NOTICE IT

Start noticing what must be present in your life and work to make it meaningful. Here are a few questions to help you reveal what may be values for you.

- What do you want your life or work to stand for? What do you want to be known for as a person and a leader? (list some adjectives)
- Notice also what makes you feel resentful or angry (it could signal a value being crossed).
- What qualities do you admire in your favorite people and want to cultivate?
- What must be present in your life or work to make it feel meaningful?
- What are your nonnegotiable actions, behaviors, and traits in your life and work?

Remember: just ten minutes per day of writing about your personal values and intentions and how your day aligns with them
produces confidence, health, and resilience–boosting effects
months, and even years, later.

TIP: You can google a list of values words or download a list at CLOSINGTHECONFIDENCEGAP.COM/
BOOKDOWNLOADS

REFRAME IT

Don't write what you think you have to do to make money or
succeed in your culture—write what is deeply important to you.
Choose words that feel deeply true for you, whether or not you,
your family, or workplace has labeled them "acceptable."

Sit with each word and notice how you react. Do you tense up
or feel drained? (Not a value.) Do you relax and feel purposeful,
excited, free, or energetic? (Likely a value for you.)

OWN IT

Claim your values. Narrow that list down to three to five. It can
help to compare similar values together and choose which feels
more freeing, energizing, or true for you.

Drop values you think you *should* have. Which values, if you
lived them, would make work and life most fulfilling for you?

> **TIP:** This activity often works best over the course of several days as you make tentative lists and notice in real time what is meaningful, what irritates you (likely a value is crossed!), and what makes you feel free and energized.

ACT ON IT

To boost your peace, your potential, and your paycheck, it's critical to know your right yeses and noes.

- What can you cut from your life or work right now because it's not in alignment with your values?
- How can you make a leadership or work decision in alignment with your values?

Visit CLOSINGTHECONFIDENCEGAP.COM/BOOKDOWNLOADS for a printable version of this tool or the entire workbook of tools in this book.

2

TAME YOUR IMPOSTER MONSTER

For so long, women and girls have been told we don't belong in the classroom, boardroom, or any room where big decisions are being made. So, when we do manage to get into the room, we are still second-guessing ourselves, unsure if we really deserve our seat at the table. We doubt our own judgment, our own abilities, and our own reasons for being where we are. Even when we know better, it can still lead to us playing it small and not standing in our full power.

I've been there plenty of times. What's helped me most is remembering that our worst critics are almost always ourselves.

MICHELLE OBAMA

When my daughter was around age four, she started to develop a condition I call the *but firsts*. When I would ask her to do something, like clean her room, she'd immediately respond with, "Mom, but first I need to _____" (get a drink, put on socks, brush my doll's hair, etc.). It would escalate near bedtime, when crawling into bed was met with several urgent *but firsts*, like getting a drink, cleaning her room (suddenly a priority!), and changing her pajamas. It was her special way of stalling or avoiding an activity that brought her discomfort.

The thing is, we never really grow out of the *but firsts*—they just get more sophisticated. Several years ago, I was sitting in a windowless gray conference room in one of those all-day corporate business meetings. As several hours stretched on, I started to become annoyed. It felt like the conversation was going in circles. Finally, we had a bathroom break. As I walked in and sat down in the stall, breathing a huge sigh of relief for a momentary change of scenery, I asked myself, *Why are you feeling so annoyed?* I had an aha moment. We'd been hearing from the same voices all day long, and it felt like a car stuck in mud. Also, most of the voices were men.

I reflected—were there mostly men in the room that day? No, while the senior leadership team was comprised of men, nearly half the room was women. I began to feel enraged. *Why don't these women speak up?* Then, almost as if the metal bathroom stall walls had a voice, I heard, *You could be the one to speak up.*

I was appalled. Who was I to speak up? I mean, I could speak up, *but first* I'd need more experience. (I'd worked there eleven years.) *But first* I'd need more confidence. *But first* I'd need to know that people wouldn't think I was stupid if I shared my idea. *But first* I'd need to prove myself, even though I'd worked in several departments with good reviews.

My grown-up version of the *but firsts* got me that day as I walked back into the conference room. I said nothing for the rest of the day and had to wrestle with my self-doubt as I continued to listen to the same voices over and over again. I was frustrated.

I knew I didn't want to spend another meeting listening to the same people and hearing mostly male voices, but I struggled to fully overcome the self-doubt that preceded speaking up in the big meeting rooms with my peers and leaders.

I wasn't able to recognize it then, because I didn't have the words for it yet, but all my "but firsts" were stemming from feeling like an imposter—the belief, despite all my work, success, and experience, that speaking up would just expose me as a fraud, and I would be "found out" that I was not as smart as they thought and totally unqualified. When I eventually changed careers, it brought new feelings of inadequacy and doubt that kept me more silent than I desired.

I didn't fully experience the cost of this doubt until I started my own business. When I left corporate America, I thought I had it all planned out—software expenses, operational expenses, marketing and licensing costs, and so on.

The biggest expense I overlooked was the cost of my thoughts.

My sophisticated *but first* thoughts sneaked back in again. The cost of these thoughts wasn't totally evident in corporate America, because despite staying more silent than I wanted in meeting rooms, or holding back on project launches until they were perfect, I still got paid every two weeks.

Running my own business, my doubt was at a whole new intensity level.

But first I have to make my website perfect before I can offer my services.

But first I have to make this coaching program perfect before I can launch it.

Before I can launch this, I need to be certain that people won't think this is stupid.

Before I can talk about my business, I need to feel more confident.

Before I can feel credible, I need to go back and get another certification.

But first, but first, but first.

All these doubtful thoughts caused me to stall, play small, not ask people to work with me, and ultimately create a scarcity mindset. And they were *expensive*. Why? Because when I was trapped in doubt and inaction, not launching my programs, not talking about my business nor asking people to work with me, I wasn't making any money. I was simply delaying revenue. This vicious cycle made me feel even more doubt, and it was ruining the potential of my coaching and speaking practice.

These thoughts were more than just doubt. They were more than just sophisticated *but firsts*. These thoughts became a mindset—an expensive mindset.

THE COST OF EXPENSIVE THOUGHTS

I didn't realize my thoughts had a price. In fact, I never used to think about what I was thinking about until I was in my midtwenties, and we had a leadership speaker and author facilitate leadership training in our organization. Best-selling author and leadership expert Cy Wakeman taught us about our ego and that most of the stressful stories we were telling ourselves—*My boss hates me, they're never going to acknowledge me, I fail when I try big ideas, people think my ideas are stupid*—are all stories that our ego has drummed up to keep us safe. The ego doesn't like discomfort or change, so it will spin lots of stories and thought tracks to keep us playing small, blaming other people, or in our comfort zone.

The problem is that most of these stories aren't true. I learned from Cy that many of my beliefs were self-made, and I could choose not to believe everything I think. I would be more productive to simply look at and take action based on the facts of a situation. This is a wise choice because according to the National Science Foundation, the average person has about twelve thousand to sixty thousand thoughts *per day*. What's even more fascinating is that 80 percent of them are negative, and 95 percent are repetitive old thoughts.

These unchecked thoughts are expensive, and if we aren't careful, they'll leave us broke. Expensive thoughts like "I'm not qualified to be here" are costly to our peace, our potential, and our paycheck.

PEACE

How do you feel in your body when you catch yourself thinking an expensive thought like this? My guess is it makes you feel doubtful, anxious, and insignificant. It likely turns your stomach, clenches your jaw, or squeezes your shoulders into your neck. It robs you of the ability to be present, calm, and confident.

POTENTIAL

What's the likelihood of taking a brave step toward your goals when you're crippled with an expensive, "I'm not qualified" thought track running through your head? LinkedIn conducted a research study that evaluated gender-based job application activity. It showed that women will wait until they meet 100 percent of the job qualifications, while men wait until they meet

60 percent before applying. Yep, it holds you back from fully expressing your potential, whether it be not applying for a job that you know you'd rock or simply keeping quiet in meetings when you have brilliant ideas that could solve big problems.

PAYCHECK

Ultimately, thoughts like this impact your paycheck. When you struggle with self-doubt, it robs you of your peace, and you show up doubtful. When you feel doubt, you play small, hide your ideas, and don't go after projects, jobs, or clients you are fully capable of handling. This impacts your paycheck as you lose out on raises you could have earned by asking. You miss out on salary bumps that you could have earned with a promotion you went for.

(PS: If you're running a team or organization, imagine what hidden expensive thoughts are swirling in your team members' heads and costing you organizational performance, revenue, or cost savings.)

DOUBT VERSUS IMPOSTER SYNDROME

When you're about to do something new or big in your life, like start a new job, take on a new project, give a big presentation, or even think about making a big career change, why does it feel like you're on the verge of being "found out?" In my experience, I was scared that if I spoke up I would be exposed as unqualified because people would think that my ideas were stupid.

My clients tell me story after story of the crippling doubt they feel when they are about ready to go into a big interview. They ask how to smother the fire of anxiety in their stomach so they can get through their big presentation successfully.

How do you know the difference between doubtful, expensive thoughts (*but first . . .*) and having imposter syndrome? The term *impostor phenomenon* was introduced in 1978 in the article "The Impostor Phenomenon in High Achieving Women: Dynamics and Therapeutic Intervention" by Dr. Pauline R. Clance and Dr. Suzanne A. Imes. The article concluded that bright, high-achieving women were carrying a persistent belief that, despite their education and many accomplishments, they felt like a fraud and that they had fooled others to believe they were smarter than they actually were. More achievements did not bring them relief from this feeling we often refer to now as imposter syndrome. In 1978, imposter syndrome was labeled an internal barrier to achievement.

As the term *imposter syndrome* has become more widely used in women's circles and workplaces, is our normal human doubt being reframed as imposter syndrome? According to *Merriam-Webster*, "doubt" is a noun, and its meaning is "a lack of confidence." Doubt is also a normal, healthy human emotion. It's human to feel doubt, and it's also likely you'll feel it any time you try something new or stretch your comfort zone. In Western society and workplaces, doubt is not fashionable. Consider this: How much time and energy does your employer spend trying to squash doubt, coach leaders not to feel or express doubt, or not allow for doubt in the meeting and decision-making rooms? Doubt is normal and healthy and keeps us humble. Many of my and my clients' best efforts were preceded by incredible bouts of doubt. It helped us prepare, rehearse, seek input, and get feed-back. I'm not sure I'd want to work for a leader who never felt or expressed any doubt—would you? Doubt is not an emotion to be cured but an emotion that can keep us curious and connected.

DOUBT

Every time I speak for women's leadership groups, I feel an overwhelming sense of doubt as I prepare my presentation. I get nervous that people will think my content is stupid. There's always a time frame when I lose confidence in my abilities to pull together a coherent message and activities in time. On the day of my larger presentations to several hundred women, I can feel more doubt creeping in. If you watch me in the corner before I go on stage, I'm pacing and drinking ice water, taking in big deep breaths. In my mind, I'm trying to quiet my thought track that this will be the event where people figure out that I have no idea what I'm talking about and that I'm a big old fraud, and they boo me off the stage. I am feeling a bit thankful, though, that I've chosen the right outfit to cover up my sweaty armpits from all the nerves. As hard as this emotion feels to experience, this doubt is healthy—it encourages me to practice my content. It encourages me to consider deeply what my audience desires and design relevant content and an enjoyable audience experience. Feeling doubt—and all its related emotions, like nervousness, insecurity, and inadequacy—keeps me humble and always curious about how I can improve my programs and speaking style.

At one of my women's leadership conferences, a participant once defined the difference between doubt and imposter syndrome best. I asked everyone at their tables, "What is the difference between doubt and imposter syndrome?" After taking some table discussion time, I asked for answers.

A woman rose her hand, "Doubt," she explained, "is a common feeling that precedes stepping out of our comfort zone, while imposter syndrome is self-sabotage." You could hear a murmur echo through the entire conference room—it was a murmur of women feeling seen and commenting in agreement of such a wise observation.

IMPOSTER SYNDROME

I agree with her, both in my own experiences and in my clients' experiences, that a persistent belief of feeling like an imposter can become a silent career killer. Imposter syndrome is the point at which the feeling of doubt has become such an expensive thought that it holds you back, sabotaging you from your full potential. In my own career, imposter syndrome kept me silent in meeting rooms, which kept me from sharing ideas that could help the organization—and in turn, help advance my career. Imposter syndrome has personally held me back from roles that I was likely qualified for, but when I saw I was missing a few qualifications, I decided not to apply. This decision left me frustrated when I saw who they did hire for the role. I knew I was just as qualified as that person.

Imposter syndrome also contributes to my clients' career sabotage; they believe they are just lucky and might be found out as a fraud if they move to a new organization. This keeps them from switching to careers that would make them happier. When they do choose to change roles or ask for a promotion, only 60 percent of women negotiate their salaries, and when they do, they ask for less than men, as Randstad Staffing research shows. I also see them holding back on negotiating their salaries, citing that they "don't deserve" to ask for more, because they are missing a few qualifications. As a former human resources professional, I can attest that men do not act this way.

Despite what you may frequently hear about imposter syndrome, you alone did not bring this upon yourself. In fact, true imposter syndrome isn't just a women's issue. Nearly 70 percent of people say they have experienced imposter syndrome at some point in their careers. The latest studies show that people reported higher imposter feelings when they are expected to have a high level of brilliance, such as in academia, or they've experienced racial discrimination, or they work in a field highly dominated by one gender and, thus, expect to be stereotyped based on their gender and the behavioral norms expected.

So imposter syndrome may not be your fault. There are systemic issues at play that organizations need to address, including creating an environment of psychological safety, inclusion, and belonging. It's important for organizations to actively deprogram racist and patriarchal norms. Many of the groups who've felt the imposter feelings have typically not seen themselves in organizational leadership teams. They haven't been represented in the rooms where decisions are made.

Before we go around diagnosing and blaming women for their lack of confidence because they have imposter syndrome, we need change in the systems that continue to promote the white male way of being, leading, and living as the primary standard of "how to be, act, and lead."

The solution here is both/and. Let's advocate to fix the system so that more diverse voices are seen and heard. And in the conversations I've had with hundreds, maybe thousands, of women, these feelings of fraudulence, luckiness, exposure—like an imposter—are real. Women feel them in their whole being.

These feelings create self-imposed limits and hesitancy at work. They keep women from showing up as their truest, fullest selves.

Let's talk about what imposter syndrome more likely is—a cluster of feelings and not a diagnosis (syndrome). Just at the moment that we get a surge of confidence or excitement about an opportunity, it feels like a little mental monster that sneaks up on us at the most inconvenient times to scare us into shrinking and playing small. The imposter monster. Most importantly, let's support women when they feel these valid feelings while we also address the systemic issues that perpetuate them.

TAME YOUR IMPOSTER MONSTER

My friend Staci is the world's funnest neuroscientist. She's not what you typically think of when you imagine a neuroscientist—there's no gray hair or dull sweater. Nope, Staci is a full-blown Texan, complete with curly dark hair, dangling earrings, and shiny turquoise necklaces. Her bubbly smile and laugh makes her southern drawl endearing and delightful. She's one smart lady.

Staci was "fixin'" to present at a neuroscience conference when I received a panicky video message from her. She told me that she'd made the mistake of checking out the list of other conference presenters and was freaking out. "I don't belong on this list, Kelli! Look at all these other people with more degrees and education than I have—they are real neuroscientists." She was mostly comparing herself to a list of older white men. "And, Kelli, my stomach is a mess—I can't sleep or eat. If I eat, it comes right out the other side. I feel like I need to withdraw from this conference. They are going to come to my session that's more lighthearted, and they're going to find out I'm just a hick from Texas who talks funny, and I have no idea what I'm doing."

Staci was feeling like an imposter. What Staci was experiencing wasn't unique; in fact, often the first place we may notice our doubt or imposter monster creeping up on us is in our body.

Once we talked her back into a good place, she went on to tell me the neuroscience of what just happened. When we feel scared, ready to stretch our comfort zone and do something new, the part of the brain that likes things to feel safe, comfy, and routine gets hijacked. This sends us into fight-or-flight mode, and our body responds accordingly. In the women I've talked to, they say this shows up as stomach issues, restlessness, heart racing, and body aches from tension. It can even perpetuate freeze mode and cause them to shut down or procrastinate so they don't have to take action—therefore sabotaging the opportunity and keeping them safe.

Staci explained that before we can move forward and get back into a more rational place the executive functioning part of our brain—that is, the part we think and act from—we first have to calm our system. One of the best ways to do this is through what US Navy SEALs call box breathing. They use this technique in high-stakes situations to get out of the fear response and back into focus. Box breathing works like this: exhale for four counts, inhale for four counts, hold for four counts, and exhale for four counts. Like I mentioned earlier, at my speaking events, you'll see me box breathing in the corner before I go onstage to calm myself. Another way to calm our system is to drink ice water, which I also have on hand during any presentation, to lighten up my red splotchy neck and make me pit out just a little bit less in my dress.

Once our body begins to calm down, we can be in the right place to check our thoughts. After talking with Staci for a while about her conference, I asked her why she was feeling so nervous. She told me that everyone else in the lineup had PhDs and were much older than her. She had a master's degree, decades of teaching experience, and plenty of awards to her name. "Why is it so bad that you don't have a PhD?" I asked.

After pausing for a moment, she replied, "I guess I don't feel qualified to be there."

The thought "I don't feel qualified to be there" is an expensive thought. It was costing Staci the peace of enjoying being part of such an impactful conference, which may cost her the potential of being asked to speak again if she didn't fully show up as herself. Ultimately, that would cost her in a future paycheck if she chose to hide her true nature and not show up as her fully expressive, educational, and energetic self.

THE RESULTS OF OUR THOUGHTS

Our thoughts can be so expensive because, as both Cy Wakeman and my Wayfinder Coach Training founder, Dr. Martha Beck, taught me, these thoughts lead to our actions, and our actions create our results. Sometimes we try to control our environment by not stretching our comfort zone or avoiding new things so that our expensive thoughts don't get triggered. Or we attempt to snuff out and ignore our feelings in an effort to boost our confidence. But the best way to shift from fear to freedom is to notice and name our emotions and make shifts in our thinking.

Let's track a thought of your own to see how it may impact your feelings, actions, and ultimately your results.

THE COSTS OF EXPENSIVE THOUGHTS

EXPENSIVE THOUGHT (EXAMPLE)	EXPENSIVE THOUGHT (COMPLETE THIS)
Trigger: a big presentation	Trigger:
Thoughts: I'm not qualified to be here.	Thoughts:
Feelings: anticipation, worry, overwhelm, insecurity, doubt, insignificance	Feelings:
Actions: procrastination to practice, hesitancy, holding back on sharing all ideas, presenting with less confidence	Actions:
Possible results: presentation falls flat, less audience connection, negative reviews, no invites to speak again	Possible results:

I bet that result feels like it escalated quickly! Was it hard for you just to pick one negative thought? If so, don't get down on yourself—it just means you are normal—and remember that our brains have a negativity bias. We may not even realize how much time we spend in negative thinking, as it's automatic. We don't tell our brains to start thinking. We wake up and the brain begins:

- What's wrong with my hair today?
- Don't screw this up again today.
- My coworker has it out for me.
- I'll never get promoted.
- They're going to see through me today and realize I'm a fraud.

And the list goes on.

Steven Hayes, author of *The Liberated Mind*, says that for most people thoughts run continuously unchecked inside our heads, and we forget that we have a choice—we can believe and buy into what these thoughts are telling us, or recognize that just because they are present, it doesn't make them helpful or true. Instead, we should *choose to fuse* with thoughts that serve us—ones that align with our values and help move us in the directions we want to go. He calls this work psychological flexibility.

Dr. Earl Miller, a neuroscientist from MIT who studies the link between fear and confidence, says that *facts ease fear*. When we are in situations in which we are feeling frozen by negative thoughts, it's helpful to examine if there's any truth behind the fear.

For example, a leader who begins a new job or big project may have a negative and recurring thought of "They're going to find out I'm a failure." Instead of sitting and ruminating on that thought, letting it impact her emotional and physical state, she could first give herself compassion that she is normal—healthy human beings have doubtful and negative thoughts. Then she could look at her evidence: *Is it true that I fail, or projects fail, when I take them on in my career?* Many times people may find evidence of one small snag or hiccup in their career when something didn't go as planned. When they make a list of evidence of their project and promotion history, what they actually find is an evidence list of success.

I also love to find evidence that the *opposite* of our negative thought is actually more true, and more freeing, than our expensive thought. Using Staci's example, her expensive thought was "I'm not qualified to be here." The opposite of this thought is simply "I am qualified to be here." The next step is to list all the reasons why she is qualified. (Spoiler alert: Staci had a long list of credentials, experience, and glowing reviews to support her qualifications—and they invited her to be there!) Notice how this empowering, freeing thought impacts how you feel in your body.

Now let's track a more freeing thought of your own to see how it may impact your feelings, actions, and ultimately your results.

THE POSSIBILITIES OF FREEING THOUGHTS

FREEING THOUGHT (EXAMPLE)	FREEING THOUGHT
Trigger: a big presentation	Trigger:
Freeing thought: I have many qualifications that earned me a spot.	Freeing thought:
Feelings: empowered, excited, ready, confident, connected, nervous	Feelings:
Actions: healthy preparation, shows up fully, shares all ideas, presents with confidence, energy	Actions:
Possible results: connects with the audience, idea exchange, builds relationships, new ideas lead to results	Possible results:

In addition, notice the difference in your body between an expensive thought and a freeing thought. One should feel more constricted and heavy. You may even notice tension in your body. A truly freeing thought should feel as such—light and open. You may even feel a bit "scare-cited"—a blend of feeling scared about a big new opportunity while also feeling the fizzies of excitement.

Next, notice that just because we have a more freeing thought doesn't mean that nerves or doubt go away—it simply allows us to recognize that emotion doesn't have to control our actions and contribute to less than desired results.

I use this exercise almost daily for those pesky, recurring talk tracks in my head—especially the *but firsts*.

YOU *ARE* QUALIFIED

There are days when no matter how much I practice my breathing work and check on my expensive thoughts, the imposter monster will just not go away. I feel rattled with nerves, I procrastinate my work, and cycle into a pit of despair that the impending event I'm nervous about will certainly be the demise of my career. In these moments, I have to pull out all the stops to tame my doubt and imposter monster.

NUMBER ONE: PULL THE PEDESTAL

In Michelle Obama's book *Becoming,* she talks about her own struggles with imposter syndrome. She reminds us just how tough imposter syndrome is because women and girls have been told we don't belong in certain places—especially where the biggest decisions are made. So even when women finally get into the room, we still second-guess ourselves and are unsure if we deserve our seat.

She shares what I believe to be one of the most liberating quotes about self-doubt and imposter syndrome: "I have been at probably every powerful table that you can think of, I have worked at nonprofits, I have been at foundations, I have worked in corporations, served on corporate boards, I have been at G-summits, I have sat in at the U.N.: They are not that smart."

Not. That. Smart. How often have you put other people on a pedestal, believing that because they've been in the role longer, have more years of working experience, or even because they exude an air of confidence, they know better than you? Because of this thought, you withhold ideas, feel heightened self-doubt, and stay more silent than you want to be. With myself and my clients, I lovingly call this *pedestal syndrome*. (I am 100 percent guilty.)

Pedestal syndrome is supported by a phenomenon called the the HiPPO Effect, which is when the highest-paid person's opinion (HiPPO), not the data, affects the decision being made. I often see this as putting people on a pedestal because they have the highest title in the room.

I know it's tempting to believe that the senior-most leaders know all the answers and that we should hold back our ideas or priorities (or even data!) because we think they know better than we do. Not only is this dangerous for the organization (refer to any corporate scandal), but this keeps our ideas and voice from being heard at work.

One thing I didn't learn until after I left corporate America is that there is nothing magical about executives, so you can take them off the pedestal. They come to coaching looking for answers too!

> It's time to stop overestimating everyone else's intelligence and underestimating your own.

NUMBER TWO: NAME THE MONSTER

Just when I think I've got this imposter monster beat, it shows up again at the most inconvenient times. It sneaks up in the weeks before I have a big presentation. It's found me the morning of a big sales call that I want to close. It's haunted me in the weeks before starting a new job. It's kept me awake at night as I work to publish this book you're reading. In these moments, I walk myself through the following steps to calm my nerves:

Notice It

First, I do the hardest thing. I summon some compassion for myself. I turn up my allowance to feel some discomfort as I stretch my comfort zone, while also tapping into my loving, compassionate self who would be offering a friend generous support, reminding them that nerves are normal, and reminding them of their unique talents.

Name It

Give it a name (there's my imposter monster again! Hey, old friend!). Giving it a name helps you effectively process and deal with feelings, according to psychologist and author Susan David. It can be even more effective if you can get granular here about the emotions you are experiencing. If you find it hard to name your emotions, google an "emotions wheel" and put your hand over your heart to tap into what you're feeling. Feeling like an imposter is often an umbrella: the emotions beneath that umbrella may be doubt, insignificance, worry, excitement, overwhelm, or others.

Normalize It

For me, whenever I'm afraid of something, it helps to remember how the thing is actually quite normal and common. This goes from watching a very calm flight attendant barely notice turbulence (so common for her!) to remembering that research shows that 70 percent of people experience imposter syndrome. Everyone experiences doubt. It is a common everyday emotion and likely means more is right with me than wrong with me.

Reframe It

When I can accurately label these feelings, I can remember what David also says, that feelings have a purpose. Remembering that my worry about giving an effective presentation signals that I want to do great work. I can also remember how much our ego doesn't like change, uncertainty, or new territory, and it is often what causes us to feel loads of doubt. In these moments, one of my favorite reframes is "This is what growth feels like—I'm stretching my comfort zone."

TODAY'S GOALS SUMMON TOMORROW'S IMPOSTER MONSTER

I've noticed a funny little thing can happen when we set big goals for ourselves. The goals we are so excited to see on our vision board often bring all the imposter feelings when they come to fruition. They activate all the *but firsts*. Every time I've set a goal of switching careers, I've been met with incredible self-doubt the evening before I started my new job. When I've celebrated booking a keynote presentation, I've been riddled with imposter syndrome in the days before I've presented. What about you?

I'm beginning to learn that a very helpful way to navigate these tough feelings is to expect them and plan for them.

Because I know I'll be a ball of doubt, overwhelm, and nerves the day before a big presentation, I plan for practice time. I include quiet time before my presentation to practice box breathing, and I'm careful about what I eat and drink so I feel my best.

While I may still struggle with my adult version of the *but firsts* when I want to accomplish another goal, I've learned two more words that may be just as impactful, but with more valuable, freeing results: *while also.*

The thing is, our normal, human emotions of doubt, worry, overwhelm will never fully go away. They're part of a healthy emotional spectrum. But feeling this way doesn't need to hold us back from showing up as our full selves, taking up the space we deserve, speaking our voice, and making an impact. It's time to stop fighting the feelings.

Have you ever noticed that the more you try to squash a feeling, the more it takes hold of you? Drop the struggle, and recognize that you can go on to do a great thing *while also* feeling unsettling emotions.

I can give a confident presentation *while also* feeling like an imposter.

I can speak up and share my ideas *while also* feeling doubtful or nervous about what people may think.

I can go for the project/promotion *while also* feeling a bit overwhelmed or unqualified.

I can have this courageous conversation successfully *while also* feeling some doubt or discomfort.

Our friend Staci the neuroscientist went on to deliver an energetic and insightful presentation that day *while also* feeling nervous and imposterish. She didn't change her approach or her topic or water down her colorful slides to blend in with the academics. She told me after the presentation that *because* her presentation was so different than the others, it was fresh and well received, leading to several additional speaking invitations from other groups. Staci is proof that you don't have to wait to feel confident before you can show up and do an amazing job—even if you are one of the only women in the room.

Remember: you won't always feel confident when you start, but taking small steps produces feelings of confidence. Sometimes you have to act into new ways of thinking and feeling because the actions of confidence come first, and then the feelings these actions generate come second. Confidence is a muscle that's built with practice and consistency. The more we practice small acts of confidence when the stakes are low, the more empowered we'll feel when the stakes are high.

When expensive thoughts lead to feelings of doubt, and possibly cause you to succumb to imposter syndrome, have compassion for yourself and remember just how common and normal this can be—especially for women in corporate who have not typically seen themselves in the rooms where decisions are made. While the systems need to change and more women need to be in senior leadership, you always have agency in making the next right choice in the career-advancing actions or changes you need to make for your own benefit, growth, or well-being. Remember: you are already more than qualified. What small step can you take today, even though you're feeling doubtful, anxious, or unqualified, to strengthen your confidence?

CLOSE THE CONFIDENCE GAP TOOL KIT

TAME THE IMPOSTER MONSTER

What would you do if you had a little more confidence?

NOTICE IT

Name the *but first* or expensive thought that's holding you back from taking action.

CALM YOUR BODY

- Have compassion for yourself and start box breathing when you notice anxious feelings.
- Drink ice water to calm nerves and overheating.

EASE YOUR MIND

- Remember: facts ease fear. Keep a "smile file"—a list or folder of compliments, well-dones, feedback, or any general love you receive from friends, coworkers, clients, and others. Organizing this into a career journal can also be helpful come interview time, when you need to recall examples of success in your career.

- **Notice** the but first or expensive thought above—is it true? What is the opposite of that thought? List evidence that the opposite is *more true* (for example, *I'm not qualified for this* versus *I* am *qualified for this*).

REFRAME IT

CONNECT TO YOUR HEART

- Slow down and break down the feelings of imposter syndrome.
- Name three or four emotions you are experiencing (google "emotions wheel" to help name these). What are these emotions signaling to you? What message do they have?

OWN IT

FLEX YOUR CONFIDENCE MUSCLE

- In this moment, remember how normal it is to feel self-doubt and imposter feelings.
- Write about a time in your life when you felt nervous, full of doubt, and like an imposter. How did you overcome it? What skills did you use? How did you get into action? What did you learn? How can you transfer those skills into your current situation?

ACT ON IT

To boost your peace, your potential, and your paycheck, it's important to get into action now and not wait to feel confident— you'll wait forever.

- What small, brave step can you take today toward your goal while also feeling a little nervous?

Visit CLOSINGTHECONFIDENCEGAP.COM/BOOKDOWNLOADS for a printable version of this tool or the entire workbook of tools in this book.

3

IT PAYS TO BE YOURSELF

Your truest self in its fullness—quirks, talents, dreams,
beliefs, all—is an irreplaceable gift to this world. It is so
beautifully and wildly gorgeous. There is no one good reason
to hide any of it. Own it, embrace it, declare it all.

JEN HATMAKER

One of my first jobs as a fresh, twenty-three-year-old career climber was calling up prospects of our bank's credit card processing service and convincing them to switch to our card processing program. If they were only allowing their customers to pay by cash or check, my job was to encourage them to sign up with us to take credit cards, which were still not commonplace in 2003 like they are today. Every day I made approximately fifty to eighty phone calls to prospective clients, which I jokingly referred to as "smiling and dialing." In reality, one-third of my time was leaving messages, one-third was hearing grumpy rants from clients who hated to be bothered with phone solicitations, and one-third was talking with someone who might be remotely interested. Despite how grueling this job was—I still say it was my worst job ever—I was good at it because I didn't mind being direct with my client and assertively asking for their business. I didn't get emotional when I got yelled at or told no. I hung up, likely rolled my eyes a bit, and just kept dialing. I met all my goals and was one of the top sales representatives.

While I'd been told by my family growing up that I was "brutally honest" and direct, I shrugged it off as just being me. Never did I imagine it could be a career liability.

My success in a sales role afforded me career advancement opportunities at my organization, first as a sales trainer, next as a professional development trainer, and eventually I was promoted to a human resources role, supporting the chief operating officer of the bank, Mike.

In one of my early days of working for him, we were winding down a long conversation about human resource policies, future organizational design, and people growth. I'd offered my insights and recommendations to him, based on best practices and feedback from employees. When meetings were over, whether the topic got boring for him or the time was simply up, he was known to wrap up abruptly, move on, or leave the room. But in this instance, he left me with this comment as he walked out of the office door. "You're not like most HR folks I've worked with," he said. "You're really direct, and many people aren't going to know how to handle you."

I'm glad he was on his way out the door because I didn't have any coherent response to that remark. I felt numb. I knew that about myself, but what do I do with that? I mean, *he was direct and people figured out how to handle him.* Why am I different? I started to overanalyze his statement. *Not like most HR people.*

Well, what should a HR person be like? What was it that I wasn't like a typical HR person? Human resources is a women-dominated field, according to Statista—over 75 percent of HR managers are women. Was I different because my qualities of a direct, no-nonsense, and unemotional woman weren't expected compared to the rest of my colleagues? While the comment left me wondering, I hadn't internalized it—yet.

Soon after, Mike nominated me to attend a three-day strategic leadership training event alongside the top leaders in his organization. I was elated, and it was the first intensive leadership training I'd ever been selected to attend. As part of the event, we received a personality assessment, the Myers-Briggs Type Indicator, and I learned I was an INTJ. The first day of the training, the facilitator conducted a deep dive of the personality assessments, revealing the meaning of the results. My type basically means that I am an introvert and prefer looking at the big picture. Not surprising to me, I lean on logic and objective information rather than emotions to communicate and make decisions. I like knowing ahead of time, and will ask for, what plans and deadlines are expected. I love time to sit and think. I also learned that this type is rare; of the sixteen possible Myers-Briggs results, an INTJ is only 1 percent of the population, and women are just less than half of that. So for women, it's the rarest type at 0.4 percent of the population. In short, I carry qualities of living, working, deciding, and communicating in a way that is typically ascribed to men. *No big deal*, I thought. I was geeking out on all this newfound self-awareness and trying to better understand my colleagues' types.

There were about twenty-five people in attendance, and I was one of four women. The remaining two days were filled what you might expect from a strategic leadership training event. We were taught strategic-planning and scenario-building tools. They taught us the essentials of managing performance, which relied heavily on finding and rewarding top performers and "high-potential" employees, while managing out low performers. The facilitators gave us sample business scenarios and observed us as we paired into groups and made business decisions and recommendations based on our assignment. They taught us the essentials of giving and receiving feedback, which on the final day we were told to plan for practicing this in "real life."

The last half of the final day, the tables in the conference room were arranged like a large square. After lunch, my twenty-four colleagues and I assembled in our seats, nervous about how the next few hours were going to unfold. I meet very few people who love giving feedback and know how to do it well. For most of us, we try to avoid it because it's uncomfortable, awkward, and vulnerable. We had to give feedback to each person in the room about their performance and behaviors over the course of the past three days, not in private, but *in front of everyone else*. (As an aside, please know I would never recommend this today as a leadership exercise.) I gave my feedback—my voice shaking as I verbalized my observations to each colleague in the format provided: what I thought they did well, and what I hoped I could see more from them.

When my turn came to receive feedback, I readied myself in my chair and hoped my racing heart wasn't giving me a splotchy neck. I thought most of the feedback to me might be suggestions on better learning the business or understanding financials, but it wasn't. The majority of the room—twenty-one men and three other women—told me that while I performed well at business analysis and making fact-based recommendations over the course of the last two and a half days, they hoped I could soften my approach in discussions while being less direct and not so opinionated in presenting my ideas. Some of my colleagues told me that my directness could be interpreted as rudeness if I wasn't careful. I felt conflicted because this feedback wasn't new; I'd been told my entire life that I was direct. But it stung in my gut and stuck like a lump in my throat because it was the first time I realized my way of being could be a liability in my career. But in my unemotional way, I armored up, stuffed it down, and nodded in agreement.

While I did learn some valuable leadership and strategic business skills in that training, necessary for any leader, I began to internalize and overanalyze a message—that my direct and no-fluff style was done serving as the asset I leveraged in a sales role and could now be a roadblock to advancement. The thought track *Are you being so direct that they can't handle it? Will they think you're rude?* ran like ticker tape through my mind for years. It still runs through my mind in social situations, when I'm coaching my clients, and as I write this book. This worry became exhausting due to the constant self-censoring and fear of what other people might think when I spoke up or discussed ideas. When I had performance reviews, my directness was always the "soft skill" development item that I needed to work on softening. My self-consciousness about it was a real confidence killer.

It took me time and study about gender biases to open my eyes to the dynamics I remembered in the room that day—that I was told to be less direct, softer, while the men were given feedback to *be more direct and assertive* in speaking up. I was too naïve to recognize it at the time, but I was penalized for the same behaviors men were congratulated for. Our chief operating officer himself, albeit someone many people enjoyed working for, had a reputation for being direct with a quick temper. People just chalked it up to him just being who he was. Mike knew the privilege afforded to him as a white male leader to be able to show up as himself at work, quick temper and all. He never struggled with my directness; maybe he appreciated it because of his own style. He took an active role in supporting my career path and teaching me insightful leadership and business lessons. Looking back now, I often wonder if his advice to me that day—*people won't know how to handle you*—was a valuable lesson he learned himself, and he was passing me a permission slip to be okay with just being me and to let others adjust. Because he, too, adjusted to my style.

While some saw my directness as a personality flaw, my self-consciousness that developed around it meant that it took me years to own it as one of my gifts and not an excuse to stay small and silent. In my later corporate leadership years, I used my "tell it like it is" style as an HR director to communicate the good, bad, and ugly to the CEO when it came to leading change, managing acquisitions, and being honest with him about what decisions would not sit well with employees. My ability to remain unemotional during times of massive organizational transitions allowed me to counsel and encourage others through their anger, resistance, and tears while also being completely transparent with people about what changes would occur with their pay, title, and benefits, even if they didn't like it. Now running my own business, I see my objective, unemotional style and directness as a competitive advantage. I can remain cool and calm in my clients' most heated and messy situations and tell them what they need to hear, not always what they want to hear. I can remain objective in watching the dynamics at play for women in organizations and cut through the noise with direct recommendations on how to address the issue. I feel more freedom to exercise my directness when I've checked in with myself and ensured that I'm speaking in alignment with my values of love and respect. In fact, many of my clients say they love that I'm "no bullshit with a ton of compassion." I'll take that as a compliment.

I've always had the sense that if I were a white male, none of my direct, unemotional style would have ever been as big a problem or a point of constructive feedback on my performance reviews. My directness would be my most celebrated leadership trait.

WOMEN ARE HELD TO A DIFFERENT STANDARD

Five years after my strategic leadership training experience, I was working for a new organization, fresh off being acquired. The acquiring company hosted a leadership development event for us, and the facilitator asked us to envision a leader. I thought of the current leaders of our organization; both our division president and the company CEO were women. She went on to display a video of images of "leaders" with inspiring music. In these image clips, there were pictures of presidents, CEOs, war heroes, and soldiers. There's no doubt they had a track record of historic leadership. The problem was, all the images were of men. They only represented about 40 percent of people in the room that day. The books recommended to us to read were definitely best sellers and great reads, but also written by white men.

Fast-forward another six years, I was talking to a client about her organization's leadership development program. She shared some of the lessons and suggested reading materials with me. I was surprised and disappointed, again, to see a list of books from all white men. They also did a "leadership image" activity, but this time some progress was made—amid all the white men they included pictures of two women. This is not about male leaders being the problem—I know them, I love them. They make wonderful leaders, and I've worked for many of them. They've written some of my favorite books, and it was a white male leader who taught me important lessons about improving diversity in leadership teams.

This is about opening our eyes to the fact that there is more than one type of ideal leadership image and style, because the gap in media representation between men and women leaders is wide. The media subtly informs and curates for us what's desirable in leaders. To be successful in the future of work, it's our responsibility as leaders, and in leadership development programs, to represent an expansive and inclusive picture of many leadership attributes. Do a google search for "leadership" and you'll be returned with stock photo images that feature mostly white men. Do another Google search for "the best leadership books" and you'll need to comb through the results to find books written by women and people of color, as most of the books returned will be written by white men. Think back to movies that feature office settings: it's most likely a white man with an all-male leadership team acting in a stereotypical assertive and controlling leadership style—the same one women are often penalized for. This represents the gap in media representation of what leadership looks and sounds like, and it perpetuates the gender stereotypes that contribute to women's likeability as leaders. It also places unfair limits on male leaders who desire to break masculine norms and lead with more sensitivity, empathy, and emotional generosity.

Ultimately, the unconscious need to conform to a certain leadership image and style keeps women from showing up authentically and diminishes their confidence.

To see more women and people of color in leadership, feeling safe to lead confidently and authentically, it's time to expand our definition of *executive presence*, which means broadening our scope of how a leader speaks, acts, believes, and carries themself. When I consult with C-level executives today, often because they want to enroll one of their women leaders in my coaching programs, it's not uncommon for them to say she needs to work on her executive presence. To this, I ask them, "How are you defining *executive presence*?" This is not always a comfortable conversation that follows as we unpack some of the deeply rooted masculine habits and norms that appear in a meeting room, what men are rewarded and women penalized for, and how they as a senior leader play a role in expanding their definition of what professionalism and presence looks like, including the presence of sensitivity and even a few tears.

In 2018 Pew Research Center published a study that revealed what Americans value, and don't value, in each gender. Characteristics that were considered valuable for women were beautiful, kind, compassionate. Characteristics that were negatively valued included power and assertiveness. Your qualities as a leader are nothing that needs fixing—society's perception needs a reality check. Gender bias for women leaders is everywhere, and a study published in the *Economic Journal* shows there is a likeability gap when it comes to women. If women aren't perceived as likeable, people will demonstrate less cooperation and less support for their efforts. The gap exists because even when men are perceived as unlikeable, they aren't penalized in terms of cooperation or support. In sum, people will be more likely to support a male leader and just accept the fact they don't like him as par for the course. This is the privilege that my former leader, Mike, enjoyed. He was quickly forgiven for his short temper and sharp words.

While women may be held to a different standard and experience likeability and representation gaps, there's mounting research that can't be ignored when it comes to women's actual leadership results. The gap is positive for women—they outperform men, not just in results but from their teams' perspective. People welcome having women as their leaders. A recent study from ResumeLab finds 38 percent of people prefer to work for a female boss, compared with 26 percent who prefer to work for a man. In a study done by Zenger Folkman, published in *Harvard Business Review*, women outscored men on 360 degree feedback reviews from their teams on seventeen of the nineteen capabilities that differentiate excellent leaders from average or poor ones.

The stereotypical gender norms, like sensitivity and emotional intelligence, made women better leaders during the COVID-19 pandemic, according to McKinsey. They did more to advance diversity, equity, and inclusion in the workplace and are better allies to people of color. Women leaders have started resource groups that are addressing the real problems working moms are facing like care options or a lack of flexibility at work. PricewaterhouseCoopers research also shows that women who work for companies with strong gender equity policies are more loyal, retention levels are higher, and these companies report higher levels of well-being.

Women are being told to "tone it down" while at the same time being told to "toughen up," but the data is clear—women make for great leaders who achieve outstanding results. Organizations who have women well represented in their C-suite recognize 50 percent more profit than those whose teams are more white and male. Many clients tell me what turns them away from job applications is seeing no women on the company leadership team. Aside from the need for representation, women leaders often enhance work culture and provide policies that benefit parents.

To bust gender likeability gaps and personality norms for women, we don't need to fix women. We need more women in leadership. In fact, the perception of women changes after companies hire female CEOs and board members, says the National Academy of Sciences in a review of over forty-three thousand business documents containing 1.23 billion words. The attitude toward women being called direct, determined, and independent improved, and it did not reduce the perception of being kind and caring. Women who demonstrate warmth, sensitivity, and collaboration were also more likely to be seen as equally competent. The bottom line of the study revealed that hiring women into leadership positions helps associate women with traits essential for successful leadership—ending gender stereotypes and removing the tightrope women walk between being competent and likeable.

If we want to make the world a better place, it begins by changing workplaces, and workplaces can be changed one woman at a time. It's time for women to own who they are and what they want, trust themselves, and know that they can be successful when they use their unique approach in alignment with their values. It creates a ripple effect and inspires other women to do the same. I can think of countless examples in which a woman broke norms to take a stand or rise up to leadership, and watching her do so unapologetically inspired me to stop hiding in some way and become more visible. Reading leadership books by powerful women paved the way for me to write this book. Watching women choose themselves and be a successful entrepreneur enabled my own entrepreneurship journey. Watching successful women executives empowered me to take the chance and go for promotions.

The world literally cannot afford women hiding, being silent, setting their aspirations aside, and following someone else's script. Because organizations are more profitable with women at the top, this is an economic issue, not a social justice issue. Even if there is backlash from people who are offended by a woman who knows her unique contributions and acts on them, owning the truth of who you are is worth it. Living in alignment with your values, showing up for yourself, and being honest about what you want is essential to our well-being because conforming is exhausting. True confidence, having faith in your abilities, is liberating. Even if it made someone else upset, I've always felt more freedom when I chose to show up as my truest self. An aligned woman is a powerful woman—she creates a ripple effect of confidence, success, and creativity that inspires other women to do the same. Think about it: Have you felt a boost of confidence and taken action because you watched another woman show up, flaws and all, and do her thing? I sure have.

WHAT'S WRONG WITH YOU IS WHAT'S RIGHT WITH YOU

There is an old bus that sits on our family farm in the middle of southwestern Nebraska. It's been parked in tall golden grass next to a large tree for the last three decades. In its prime, it was periwinkle blue on the bottom and white on top, but now, rust has taken over, adding a dose of bronzing that crawls across the sides. It's quite the sight and reminds me of my great-grandma Elizabeth every time I see it. In the 1960s, she bought this bus so she could pick up and house a seasonal harvest crew for her one-thousand-acre farm and ranch. While this might seem like "so what?" in today's world, remember that in the 1960s many wives were homemakers. Women just didn't buy buses and run farms—they couldn't even borrow money without a male relative's cosign until 1974—but she did just that while her husband worked days and nights away on the railroad; she continued to do so even after her husband passed when she was only sixty years old.

Elizabeth landed her first job as a teenager working in her parents' hardware store. She ran the cash register, provided customer service, helped with marketing, and managed the books. In that job, her dad trusted her to run the show, so from a young age she learned valuable business skills. She understood how margins worked and how businesses bought a product for one price and resold it for another. She came to understand human behavior, how people made buying decisions, and good customer service standards. She learned how to negotiate, not just with vendors but with customers. She knew how much everything cost and developed incredible math skills. She went on to attend college around 1915, equally as unusual for a young woman. These skills rendered her extremely intelligent, hard to fool; she could size up people quickly.

She was married to a railroad engineer and had one son and two daughters. While most women would stay home, she was not content to do so. She made it through the Great Depression by relentlessly saving money—she knew the value of every penny. In the late 1940s, with this money saved, she made a large cash down payment on the family farm, and she, with her husband's cosign, borrowed the rest of the money to fund it. To run this farm successfully, she had to be shrewd. She primarily raised my dad when he was young, and he would tag along with her to business deals—where she negotiated everything from $75,000 tractors and $350,000 combines (today's dollars) to nickel-and-diming the people in the parts store for farm supplies. She knew her numbers. She knew the soft and hard costs of things. Sadly, when she was widowed in 1960, it meant she had to pay with cash for everything from farm supplies to the bus—the bank wouldn't give her a loan as a single woman. She still saved enough money to cover crop losses in bad years so she wouldn't have to spend money on insurance. She made direct eye contact with people, asked for what she wanted, and would stand there silently until she got her way. When she walked into a store, the employees immediately knew it was easier just to go grab the boss, because Elizabeth was there to negotiate to the lowest dollar.

While she was small in stature at four-foot-eleven, her reputation was big. People called her shrewd, intimidating, confrontational, bossy, a bitch. According to society at the time, there was a long list of things "wrong" with her simply because she was a woman. She wasn't concerned with conformity or making you feel comfortable. She didn't back down; however, Elizabeth was respected, because over time she forged relationships built on fairness and trust. She admitted often that people didn't like her at first, but over time people came to respect her directness. She had many ranch hands who walked off the job, but she built lasting relationships with the ones who saw through to her passionate and genuine heart. It wasn't important for her to be the most popular but to have a small set of friends she could play bridge with when she wanted a girls' night. Her motive was never to hurt people but to see both sides get a fair deal. If there was a chance you were being taken advantage of, she was the woman you wanted in your corner to fight for you.

Elizabeth was admired as an astute businesswoman—someone who was tough and fair, and it paid off. Upon her death, she'd built a thriving farming business despite the inability to borrow money, and she'd endured the difficulties of being a widow and losing her son when he was twenty-one. Yet she'd built a legacy for her family. When they went through her safe-deposit box after her death in 1981, they found $300,000 in cash rolled up inside—all those pennies pinched and saved, meant to be an inheritance for her two daughters. She was determined to be self-sufficient and encouraged her family to be the same.

I imagine today she could tell us many stories about things she did because she didn't listen to the cultural messages of "women shouldn't do that." I'm certain that if someone told her she couldn't do it, she likely would have done just that plus 20 percent more. I know so many women who are bold and ready leaders, just like her, who have no problem turning chaos into grand, creative outcomes. These same women are often told they are aggressive, bossy, or too direct and experience liability bias in the workplace.

She did not conform to gender stereotypes then, and still would not today. Have you ever been told you are too _____? Even women who may fit more traditional gender norms, and might find themselves the opposite of Elizabeth, still struggle with being labeled as too emotional, sensitive, or people pleasing.

But what if your "flaws" are actually your greatest gift? Because my great-grandma was bold, shrewd, and assertive, she created a farm and business that employed workers and created growth and needed services in her community. She clothed, cared for, and put food on the table for her family. The corn and wheat grown on her farm served hungry families. She was five decades ahead of her time, but her story reminds me that we have permission today to stop conforming who we are to make someone else more comfortable.

First, consider this. What if all the qualities you've been scared to demonstrate are exactly what you need to be successful? Try this reframe.

Because I am _____, I am able to _____.

Because I am sensitive, I can read the needs of our team.

Because I am assertive, I tackle hard challenges most people shy away from.

Because I am direct, I am clear in communicating needs and outcomes.

Sometimes it can be hard to find the good in what you per-ceive to be a flaw. Try on these reframes and see what aligns best for you:

IF THE CRITICISM IS THAT YOU ARE:	MAYBE THE TRUE GIFT IS THAT YOU ARE:
Critical, Micromanager	Principled, Having Integrity
Soft, People-Pleasing	Empathetic, Rewarding
Competitive, Aggressive	Focused, Efficient
Emotional, Sensitive	Authentic, Purposeful
Direct, Unemotional	Objective, Innovative
Unrealistic, Scattered	Visionary, Creative
Bossy, Controlling	Decisive, Influential
Quiet, Indecisive	Genuine, Inclusive

Second, remember that anyone can be a great leader if they own what makes them amazing and use it in a healthy way to create change, positively impact others, and get results that matter. I've worked with leaders at all levels across the country, and the best leaders are self-aware leaders. A key part of growing yourself, and your team, is leading with your unique approach *while also* aligning your approach with your values.

My unique approach _____ + a value of mine _____.

I am _____ and _____.

Situations where this approach is needed in my work-life:

_____

You can be:

- Direct and genuine.
- Sensitive and courageous.
- Assertive and loving.
- Bold and respectful.
- Emotional and balanced.

Are you part of a leadership development program that helps you cultivate your unique gifts, or are you spending your energy working to be more like your CEO, boss, or admired colleague? What would serve you best in the long run for your health, happiness, and success?

> Stop conforming and start confidently choosing yourself—when you spend your energy trying to show up like someone else, you lose the power that makes you **you**.

CHOOSE YOURSELF

Shannon and I worked together for a long time, both as colleagues and eventually in a coaching relationship. Shannon consistently received the feedback that she was too conflict-averse and then suddenly emotional in high-stakes moments. By the time we'd reconnected, she was crispy with burnout. She felt completely unseen at work. She felt like she was working so hard to show up and conform to the behaviors that were valued in the organization—trying to be more extroverted, assertive, and direct, all of which were demonstrated by her direct leader and many of the C-level executives. She had a feeling that the organization wasn't a long-term fit for her, and she said, "Kelli, I don't even know who I am anymore. I feel like I'm invisible and pushing a rock uphill every day." Before she made any career changes, she tried to communicate with her leader on what she wanted and needed in her role. In these conversations, she'd feel embarrassed because tears would just pour out unexpectedly.

She admitted to me, "I'm so sensitive to feelings, conflicts, and personal dynamics, and I *hate this* about myself! Why can't I just be tough and direct in conversations where I need to hold my own?" Shannon was sensitive, and this was her gift, but she wasn't totally bought in yet. We dug into her work history, and Shannon reflected on the projects in which she excelled the most: change management, employee experience, working through mergers, and executing new product campaigns. She valued harmony, balance, generosity, health, and family. When I asked her *why* she excelled at those projects, and encouraged her to ask former colleagues for feedback on her unique contributions, the evidence was overwhelming:

Shannon excels at leading others through change because she's empathetic and can see all sides.

Shannon pulls together big groups and builds consensus because she knows how to find common ground.

Shannon is excellent at launching product campaigns because she builds great relationships with every stakeholder in the process—she knows what they need.

Shannon's sensitivity wasn't a liability; she was excellent and well regarded by colleagues *because* she was sensitive.

This was such a huge aha to her that she didn't need to be

more like her boss or other leaders to be successful—she needed to own the skills that she had worked so hard to avoid. She said that once she owned her sensitivity, stopped hiding it, and more readily voiced her needs and viewpoints on behalf of it, she actually became *less teary-eyed* in meetings. Soon after, she decided to pursue a new role at an organization, and she reached out to me again. "What's the best way to be in interviews so that I'll get hired?"

I gave her the same advice I learned myself and give to my other clients: "Be yourself."

This might seem counterintuitive. When you are interviewing for a job or hoping to be selected for a big project, you should figure out what the selection committee wants and act accordingly, right? Wrong, according to research by Francesca Gino at Harvard. In a study, she found that people who behaved authentically (versus catering to what they thought people wanted) were 26 percent more likely to be hired. Objectively, this makes sense—can't you seem to snuff out when people *aren't* behaving authentically? I can. Besides, pretending is exhausting, isn't it? I'm convinced that many of us are burnt out because we're working harder at conforming to certain qualities defined as "likeable" or "promotable" than we are being ourselves. If they hire the *pretend you* in the interview process, then you'll need to pretend for the remainder of your employment. You will be constantly adjusting who you need to be instead of letting others adapt to and love the true, brilliant you. What a confidence killer.

In more ways than one, it pays to be yourself. Shannon decided to be open and honest during the interview process—she was sensitive, and that was her superpower. Because she was sensitive, she was successful in building consensus and deep trust, and she brought groups together to achieve a common goal. She was hired, of course; who doesn't want that type of leader in their organization? And now in her role, she feels so much *ease*. Not only because she loves the work but also because she's let herself off the hook to conform to a more masculine leadership approach, or any leadership approach that doesn't align with her unique leadership style.

It pays to be your authentic self. There is no one ideal leadership style—anyone can be a great leader if they're willing to own who they are and have the confidence to use their unique approach.

CLOSE THE CONFIDENCE GAP TOOL KIT

IT PAYS TO BE YOURSELF

NOTICE IT

Where might you be self-censoring or holding back so you don't show up a certain way?

OWN IT

What have I always been told about my personality while growing up or in a professional environment? Examples: "You're too sensitive . . . You're too bossy . . ."

REFRAME IT

How is that trait a unique gift rather than a liability? What does it allow me to do?

Because I am _____, I am able to _____.
I am _____ and _____.

> **TIP:** Remember: There are many styles of leadership. Anyone can be a great leader if they're willing to show up as their best self. Refer back to the suggested reframes earlier in this chapter.

EVALUATE THE FEEDBACK

How do I discern credible feedback from a trusted source on my approach versus feedback intended to keep me defaulting to expected gender norms?

ACT ON IT

To boost your peace, your potential, and your paycheck, it's time to stop hiding behind your unique qualities and use them for impact.

List examples, personal and professional, of when your unique quirks have created a successful outcome. Why did your approach make the difference? How can you transfer this into a current situation? How will you stop hiding behind your unique gifts and show up to use them today?

Visit CLOSINGTHECONFIDENCEGAP.COM/BOOKDOWNLOADS for a printable version of this tool or the entire workbook of tools in this book.

4

ALIGN YOUR PURPOSE AND YOUR PAYCHECK

Happiness comes from being who you actually are
instead of who you think you are supposed to be.

SHONDA RHIMES

'd spent eleven years at the bank, which was the first company to hire me when I was looking for a job while trying to relocate back to Nebraska after taking my first job after college at an investment firm in Missouri. I needed a paycheck, so I took it. In the eleven years I spent there, I'd worked in nearly every department—investments, smiling and dialing to sell credit card processing, and retail banking. I'd been featured in their television commercials and print ads. I'd moved up from a salesperson to a sales trainer, and from human resources advisor to overseeing training and development for the retail banking operation in six states.

Training was my passion. I had an outstanding team that weathered the banking crisis of 2008. We had our six-figure budget stripped while still providing training for the entire company during a reorganization. We got creative and built out our own professional development and customer service programs that were so impactful they won a national award from *Training* magazine, a huge accomplishment in our field. In spite of all of this, I grew tired of hearing no to new programs, running on a shoestring budget, and the slow pace of serving up the new training offerings we dreamed up because of the layers of approvals needed. I thought I was ready to learn something new. A colleague encouraged me to apply for a role in the marketing department. Having always had an interest in marketing, I went for it, and accepting the role meant a big boost to my salary—I'd be earning close to six figures, which was a goal of mine.

Just like the other role changes I'd made in the bank in my first eleven years, the first few months in the role were exciting. I was learning new things and meeting new people. I was enjoying my fatter paycheck. But as the weeks went on, I found myself frustrated again with the slow pace of the work, the layers of red tape and approvals to get anything done, which had been a theme in all my roles there. My time was spent doing more operations and technical project work than creative marketing work. The new-job smell had worn off, and I was bored. Again.

As the weeks stretched on, I found myself peeking once again at the internal job boards, and it hit me—this was a cycle. I was not happy, and I couldn't figure out why. Why did I keep getting bored so quickly after landing new roles? How did I even get to this moment—doing things at work that always felt monotonous? I realized I couldn't keep department hopping at this organization. I had to dig deeper.

On my commutes home, my inner critic got noisy: "There must be something wrong with you. This is a best place to work for working mothers. They are a pillar of excellence in the community. People want to work there. They have admirable core values and community standing. You just need to grind it out and get your shit together."

For a while, that's what I did, but I felt even more exhausted. For the first time I wondered, *Is it time to leave the organization altogether?* I was scared to death at the thought of this. This organization had literally raised me. My coworkers saw me get married, have a baby, go through miscarriages, get divorced. Many of my friends and people in my social circle worked there.

My self-doubt hit hard with questions like:

- What if all my success at this organization has been luck, and I will fail anywhere else?
- What if I leave and my new company exposes me for the fraud that I truly am, and I can't hack it anywhere else?
- Who was I without this company?
- Who was I if I couldn't say I worked there?
- Who was I without my title, salary, and benefits?

The pain and discomfort of all this uncertainty burned like fire in my stomach at the thought that this era of my life could be over. So I did what I always resort to when I'm panicked and out of answers: journal and take lots of walks. I read every article I could find about changing careers and finding work you love to do. This helped me create a career alignment check of sorts and get clear on five things:

1. While the organization had a noble purpose in the community and had won many awards, money was a fascinating concept to me, but the business of credit cards and checking accounts was not.

2. I didn't feel like I was able to use my unique talents most of the time. Many of the things that I loved doing, that made me feel in flow and energetic, like developing new training and leadership programs, often weren't in budget.

3. My energy level on the close of most business days was low, not because of the people but because of the amount of bureaucracy and red tape I had to work through. Things did not move fast, and innovation was often met with skepticism.

4. I didn't agree with how the organization made decisions. I didn't love how they advocated that they were a great place to work for working moms, but they had no women in their senior leadership team.

5. Coupled with some initial clarity I had on what my career nonnegotiables were at that point in my life, I knew they didn't value creativity, innovation, and learning like I did. I wanted to test and learn without constantly working around compliance rules.

Although I was frustrated, I realized I couldn't just leave for leaving's sake. While I'd decided for myself that life was just too short to do work that drains me, I didn't want to keep repeating this pattern. If I wasn't clear about what I truly wanted, and found work that I truly loved, then I'd be repeating this pattern every twelve to eighteen months for the rest of my life. My career looked great on paper up to that point, but I felt like I was pushing a rock uphill on the daily, which left me full of doubt.

If you're also feeling this way, you are not alone. The pandemic that started in 2020 caused many women to reevaluate what truly mattered and how to align their work to better fit their lives and desires. For the first time, women stopped to ask themselves, *Is this even worth it?* At one point in the fall of 2021, 65 percent of employees were looking for a new job, according to a poll of 1,007 full- and part-time US workers conducted by PwC. That was nearly double the 35 percent of workers who said they were seeking new work the previous May.

According to the 2021 McKinsey Women in the Workplace report, 40 percent of women considered leaving their company or switching jobs, primarily due to burnout and the toll the ongoing pandemic took on their personal and professional lives. Many women found themselves at a career crossroads and wanted to do something more meaningful and purposeful with their life, something that used their unique gifts.

New job circumstances won't always make us happier in the long term, especially if we bring in the same old habits that created our current frustrating situation. We may unknowingly end up recreating dissatisfaction in our new role, which contributes to a confidence roller coaster. If you're wondering if you're in the right role and want to ensure a future role is a good fit, it might be time to take a career alignment check.

TAKE YOUR OWN CAREER ALIGNMENT CHECK

1. Am I passionate about the company's purpose and who they serve?
2. What's my energy level on the close of most business days?
3. Does 80 percent of my work make me feel in flow? Creative? Maximize my talents?
4. Is the work aligned with my greater career intentions and goals?
5. Do my values align with the company's values and decisions?

If you answered low or no to most of these questions, it might be time to do a deeper evaluation on if you are in the right career.

HOW TO KNOW WHAT ROLE IS MEANT FOR YOU

Jill Ellis's early career tenure had no indications of ever becoming one of the world's most successful soccer coaches. She grew up on the southern coast of England as a soccer fan, even though she couldn't play organized soccer as it was considered "unladylike" in 1970s Britain. Being naturally athletic, she would tag along with her brother and play with the boys whenever they needed an extra player. In 1981 the Ellis family moved to the States, to Virginia, where her father founded a soccer academy. She began to play formally in high school and then in college at William & Mary.

She earned her bachelor's and master's degrees and had a lucrative career as a technical writer for a major technology company. But she longed to play soccer. She would find every opportunity to play and coach in her community. Growing up in England, coaching soccer wouldn't have been a viable career path, but now in the United States, she knew she had options, and she couldn't help but follow what brought her alive. Ellis's former college coach, April Heinrichs, invited her to be her assistant at Maryland, and she accepted. Realizing that coaching was her true gift, she left her high-paying career in tech for just $6,000 in annual salary as a university assistant. Jill said, "I had to choose my passion over my paycheck." Her mother was horrified and her father, John, encouraged her to "do something substantial" instead.

Well, she did just that. She quickly accelerated her soccer coaching career and became a legendary coach, the winningest soccer coach *ever* in US history. She coached the United States women's national soccer team from 2014 to 2019, winning two FIFA Women's World Cups in 2015 and 2019, making her the second coach to win consecutive World Cups. Her ending salary was $291,029, which is much better than $6,000, but unfortunately eleven times *less* than the head coach of the never-as-successful US men's soccer team. Jill chose passion over paycheck but illustrates this: she ultimately aligned her purpose and her paycheck. Her talents, her true purpose in life to accelerate the game of soccer and coach women, ultimately became a sustainable paycheck.

Your purpose can align with your paycheck, too, if you're willing to take a leap of faith.

So how do you know what work is meant for you? I started where Jill did, and you can too. I reflected over the course of my entire career to that point and paid close attention to work that I was drawn to, work that I could not stop dreaming about. I, too, took a part-time job teaching at a university because it felt *fun*, not because the pay was worth it. I felt confident walking into the classroom. Noticing that it felt fun could be my first clue, I asked myself some questions to gain more clarity into my unique talents—the things I'd been put on this Earth to do:

- What work made me feel most like *me*?
- What projects felt exciting and energizing—like the work was effortless?
- Where did I feel the most challenged in a way that brought out the best version of me and my talents?
- What could I geek out about all day long?
- What types of projects did I long for or continually search and ask for?
- What do people say I have a gift for, or what help or advice do they come to me seeking?
- What work aligns not just to my talents but to my values?
- Ask others: What do I do better than anyone else you know? (Others can sometimes see this more clearly than you because your talents often feel effortless.)

In this reflection, I was noticing in my body the times in my career that felt easy, natural, and fun. Effortless yet magnetic. Like Jill, I noticed what I couldn't help but get myself into. Hers might be soccer, but mine was teaching, training, and building new leadership development programs for organizations, especially during major changes. I was always finding myself in that role, which felt confident and fun. Notice where you feel like you're pushing a rock uphill—heaviness, dread, and exhaustion in your body are an indication you aren't using your talents.

Once I combined my career alignment check questions and the unique talents questions above, I made the following career purpose statement:

I will find a career that uses my talents of educating and inspiring others to do their best work by using their talents.

I will follow my passion of learning and education and find a career that promotes balance and my value of continuous learning.

I will choose and live purposefully in alignment with my values of love, respect, and family. I will slow down, respect balance, and think of meaning. I will adequately provide for my daughter and me.

I will create a foundation for thought leadership and change. To write, teach, and replicate educational opportunities.

WRITE YOUR OWN CAREER PURPOSE STATEMENT

- I will find a career that . . .
- I will follow my passion of . . .
- I will choose and live purposefully in alignment with my values of . . .
- I will create . . .

I believe that so many women are frustrated and burned out today not just because of heavy workloads but also because they do work that doesn't fuel their fire; it just bores them to death. Life is too short to do work that drains you, and no amount of money is worth the misery. Doing the work to name and claim your talents helps you not only identify your strengths but can help you reveal greater purpose in your career.

> The more clearly you see your own talents, the more clearly you can see the talents of others without the confidence-killing effects of compare-and-despair.

Gallup research says that people who use their strengths every day are six times more likely to be engaged at work. It reduces burnout, and people are less likely to leave their job. Gay Hendricks, author of *The Genius Zone* and *The Big Leap*, says that working in your "zones of genius" allows your creativity to flow freely. His research and experience shows that people who actively pursue the things that offer them fulfillment and satisfaction make their work and career sustainable, and yes, it is ultimately lucrative.

Claiming your talents likely leads you to ask the next question: If I've been given these talents, don't I want to be purposeful about using them in my life and work? According to McKinsey, a research and consulting firm, nearly two-thirds of US-based employees said enduring the COVID-19 pandemic has caused them to reflect on their purpose in life, and nearly half said they are reconsidering the kind of work they do as the pandemic progressed. This isn't surprising—they found that 70 percent of the employees say their sense of purpose is largely defined by work. And as the pandemic stretched on longer than most people imagined, it caused many to pause and determine if their work is truly aligned with their values or their talents or is even making them happy.

They also found that people who live their purpose at work are more productive than people who don't. They are healthier, more resilient, and more likely to stay at the company. Also, McKinsey found that when you work for an organization whose purpose and values are aligned with yours, you're more likely to be engaged, loyal, and recommending that your friends come work with you as well.

START NOTICING YOUR ENERGY

In my own experience, and in working with my clients, perhaps an even simpler way to uncover your unique talents is to notice your energy. Have you ever noticed that when you're working on something you love, you lose track of time? Your energy is off the charts, it comes alive, and you can't wait to dig in. This is a huge clue as to what is a unique talent for you and that you're meant to use it on purpose. I find that our work tends to fall into one of three buckets:

ENERGY SUCKERS

These projects feel like they take heroine effort, even though the task wasn't all that large or difficult. As you were doing a certain type of project, did it feel heavy and constrictive? Energy suckers are those projects that we may be fully capable of doing, but they zap our joy. Someone else can likely do them better—in fact, this is likely someone else's unique talent (so why keep it from them?).

ENERGY STALLERS

These projects are tricky because they throw your energy into neutral. You don't feel drained while doing them, but they don't ignite your energy either. You're good at these tasks, situations, or projects—in fact, you may have a higher level of ability than most people. Because you are competent at them, people may summon your help to do these projects often. But when you're doing them, you feel like there is a part of you left unexpressed. In this bucket, your gut may be nudging you that there is something in you that's overlooked and underutilized. Still, while you're good here, it's someone else's best talent. In fact, this is where a woman often gets trapped in the "golden handcuffs"—working for excellent pay and benefits in a job that's "pretty okay" but too scared to find something that truly lights her up and aligns with her values because she's worried that she can't match the money or benefits she currently enjoys. Long term, this eats away at confidence.

ENERGY SURGERS

These projects are the sweet spot you're looking for. These projects bring a paradox—they are challenging, but they make you feel amazing, in flow, and as your most creative self. You could work on these projects for hours and lose track of time. Working on these projects feels effortless, and when you're done, your energy is *better*, not worse. They feel easy, fulfilling, and even fun, even though they may be challenging. Hence, they surge your energy—you feel light and free and still have your best self left after work to be engaged with your hobbies, friends, and family.

Where are you spending the most of your time at work today? Where should you be spending your time? What would be different for you in your career and in your confidence if you could spend the majority of your time working with your energy surgers? Can you feel the difference in your body? You were not created to do work that drains you; that's why noticing your energy and the clues your body gives are so important in creating a career you love.

WORK PROJECTS BREAKDOWN:
WHERE IS MY TIME SPENT?

Energy Suckers	Energy Stallers	Energy Surgers
_____%	_____%	_____%

The next question my clients ask is "Is it truly possible to stay in your energy surger bucket when people are telling you what to do at work?" The short answer is yes, but it can take some work. Also, you don't always need to change careers to find work that's better suited for you. I recommended evaluating your current role first to see where you can feel more energized. Specifically, spending more (ideally most) of your time in the energy surger bucket requires three things: reflection, consistency, and advocacy. Let's unpack those briefly.

Reflection: Take the time to observe your energy, and notice if a project is an energy sucker, energy staller, or energy surger—for you.

Consistency: Tasks creep in. Every quarter—or what feels right to you—take notice what's on your plate and how it aligns to your talents and impacts your energy. Then dump, delegate, or outsource the work that's sucking your energy.

Advocacy: You communicate clearly to your boss and peers what your strongest talents are and what type of work you'd most like to take on. This may not happen overnight but through consistent conversations at work. The good news is that several of my clients have stayed at a company they loved and redesigned their roles into something more enjoyable simply by having this energy and talents conversation with their leader.

Being clear about your talents to yourself is one thing, but sharing them with someone else feels vulnerable because it opens the door for critique. What if you share what you love to do and are met with well-meaning criticism that your talent is not marketable or practical? Or what if people don't agree with your self-assessment and tell you that you aren't as talented as you think? You're right—not everyone may see the possibilities like you do, and that's why paying attention to your energy is so important. Trust yourself. What good is claiming your unique talents and then hiding them, hoping that your boss or peers will see this gift in you and bring it to life? People are horrible guessers as to what will be uniquely successful for you, so your role is advocating for the gift that's been given to you. If you don't do it, then who will?

Is it possible to find a career that allows you to *only* work in your energy surger bucket? No. Author Mark Manson says it best. When someone asks him about the best career for them, he responds with, "What's your favorite flavor of shit sandwich?" While gross to think about, it's true. Every job will have tasks that you won't want on your plate—the key is to find a role that allows you to spend 80 percent of your time surging your energy. Some work will stall you in neutral, but only a small percentage should suck your energy. In a best-case scenario, you are happy to eat that crap sandwich because it's worth the joy you feel 95 percent of the time in your career. As a self-employed coach, trainer, and speaker, I feel energized by my work 90–95 percent of the time and happily eat my gross sandwich of reconciling my numbers at the end of every month so I can continue to confidently work in a career I love. I just add a side of chocolate to make it more enjoyable.

OWNING YOUR TALENTS IS THE ANTIDOTE TO IMPOSTER SYNDROME

Tara was like many women during the pandemic—a highly motivated leader in her technology organization trying to juggle working from home during the pandemic, with a partner who traveled frequently, while taking care of a young child. She was happy, but she wanted more—more challenging work assignments, work that better aligned with her talents. She was tired of seeing people getting promoted to jobs she would love to have.

She gained the courage to apply for a huge promotion. When she earned it, she negotiated the time and schedule she needed for good work-life rhythm, along with the salary she desired.

But there was a confidence gap. She told me that for the longest time she didn't feel like she truly belonged in the room among her new, higher-level colleagues. Even when she earned a promotion that was in alignment with her strengths and talents, it didn't cure the feeling of not belonging; it actually made it worse because she had new levels of visibility and access to senior leadership. She felt scared she was going to walk into the new role, new meetings, and not deserve to be there, and thus remain silent and not contribute her leadership or ideas.

"Imposter syndrome is exactly what I had," she told me.

One of the tools we worked on together was discovering and owning her talents so she could align her purpose and her paycheck. She did several weeks of reflection on the types of work that made her come alive. She reflected on the types of projects that she not only excelled at but loved doing. She asked her trusted friends and peers what they perceived to be her best gifts, her strengths, and what she could do better than anyone else.

Once she finished her discovery and reflection work, she wrote down and claimed her themes of advocacy, program building, gathering support, innovation, and boldness. She made a career purpose statement. Tara communicated the themes to her boss and asked for more projects in alignment with those themes.

She says it best: "I learned to own what makes me amazing, effective, and recognized my strengths at a deeper level. This helped me exponentially by overcoming my imposter syndrome, because now when I walk into a room, I am confident in what I bring to the table and the expertise that I bring. I know what I am capable of contributing. Now, I'm leading a team, projects, and initiatives that I would have never been bold enough to take—I would have deferred them to someone else. I am loving where my career is now."

TAKE A RISK ON YOUR TALENTS

It's easy to fall in line with saying yes to what our leaders ask of us. First, it feels good to be asked, and oftentimes we don't want to disappoint someone, so we say yes. Second, we're often told messages that doing what we truly love is great, but there's no money in it, so it's better to follow the safe, salaried, and benefitted path—this was a big problem for me.

One of the things that is slowly killing women is that we've spent too long conforming to who we think we're supposed to be or doing work we think will make us successful. We don't spend enough time noticing and using our unique talents. Getting clear on your talents requires you to trust yourself and own what you've been put on this earth to do. Then it requires the courage to tell people about your talents and say no to everything that's getting in the way of using them.

I'll be honest: the best job move I ever made included a pay cut. From the moment I knew it was time to leave the bank after eleven years, I committed to getting clear on my talents and career purpose. I also knew a change wouldn't happen overnight, so I had to learn how to stay and work in alignment with my values while also looking for the right next move, which realistically might take up to one year.

In my journal, I wrote down my talent themes, my career non-negotiables, and what I wanted to accomplish in my career via my career purpose statement so I could look for the role I wanted. When I went in for interviews, I was unapologetic about my strengths and the types of things that made me want to geek out. I was clear about what I loved and didn't love. This might feel risky during a job interview—after all, don't you want them to like you and hire you? I felt it was more of a risk to *not be clear*. What if they hired the fake me, and then I'd have to follow through on that? I held the mindset that I wanted someone to hire me for who I truly was, not who they were making me up to be. If they hired me flaws, talents, and all, then I could show up to work and not have to live up to be someone I was not.

After about nine months, I found a role as the director of talent management for a technology organization—essentially, I oversaw human resources. I showed up to each interview as my true self, and when one of the assignments was written responses to career and leadership questions, I decided to risk geeking out too much by making an infographic instead of just writing long form text. Showing information graphically was a talent for me, and it felt easy and fun. I figured it would be a great way to eliminate that employer as a career option if they didn't appreciate my creativity. About five minutes after submitting my assignment, I got an email back from the owner of the firm, and she said they'd been looking for someone for years who could take boring information and make it visually beautiful and easily communicated to others. I was hired.

It felt good to be rewarded for taking a risk on my talents. Yes, I took a pay cut, but it was worth it because it provided many complementary benefits. The people, culture, and work were fun. I loved my career there—every day, even the hard ones, still felt challenging and fulfilling. Until the point we were acquired by a new firm, my energy was back and higher than ever. I am convinced that because this role allowed me to show up as my best self every day and use my gifts and helped my purpose become a reality I was able to get a pay raise a few months posthire and was making more than at my previous role. So a short-term pay cut resulted in a longer-term pay raise when I bet on myself and talents, not unlike the journey that Jill experienced.

Using your talents pays—not only in your paycheck but in your energy and ability to just be the best, most quirky, and gifted you every day. It pays in your confidence because, like Tara explained above, when you are clear on what you bring to the table, you spend less time in "compare and despair" with people around you. Instead of ruminating over all the things you are not, you can quickly recall the value you bring. Every moment you spend in comparison, you waste your gifts and kill your confidence. Ultimately, using your talents gives you a sense of purpose you can align with your paycheck.

CLOSE THE CONFIDENCE GAP TOOL KIT

ALIGN YOUR PURPOSE AND YOUR PAYCHECK

OWN IT

Claim your purpose and your talents. For help, refer back to the questions at the beginning of this chapter.

My unique talents: _____

My career purpose statement: _____

NOTICE IT

Sometimes noticing what surges your energy gives you clues into your unique talents. Struggling to clarify your unique talents? Sometimes it's easier to list what they *aren't,* so don't overlook making a list of things you're doing at work that are energy suckers or stallers.

Energy Suckers	Energy Stallers	Energy Surgers
_____ %	_____ %	_____ %

ACT ON IT

To boost your peace, your potential, and your paycheck, it's critical to advocate for and use your talents:

- What conversations do I need to have with my leader or colleagues to share my unique talents and discuss how to incorporate them at work?
- In what ways could I be scared of letting my real talents be seen—am I carrying any old messages about not wanting people to know them? (that is, criticized for them in the past)
- What's a task I can dump or delegate today that's sucking my energy?
- If I didn't care what anyone would think, what's one small way I'd use a unique talent of mine today?

Visit CLOSINGTHECONFIDENCEGAP.COM/BOOKDOWNLOADS for a printable version of this tool or the entire workbook of tools in this book.

5

LEAD MORE BY DOING LESS

"Restore connection" is not just for devices, it is for people too. If we cannot disconnect, we cannot lead. Creating the culture of burnout is opposite to creating a culture of sustainable creativity. This is something that needs to be taught in business schools. This mentality needs to be introduced as a leadership and performance-enhancing tool.

ARIANNA HUFFINGTON

H eather is a rising star in her firm. She went to school for law and knew early on in her life that she wanted to be a lawyer. After a few roles in small private firms, she developed a solid client base but was looking for more. She received accolades for being so popular with clients, but she wanted to move to a firm where she had the opportunity to become a partner. After some job searching, she found an opportunity with a growing firm that promised a path to partnership, so she took it.

And, of course, Heather was beloved by her clients. Any time a skilled professional switches firms, there's a risk that clients won't follow, but not Heather's clients. They all followed her, and she kept them all, even with her growing responsibilities. In just over one year, she began managing the firm's local branch location of legal and office professionals. She also became the firm-wide expert on complex business mergers and acquisitions. In less than three years, Heather became a partner.

You'd think that Heather would be ecstatic about achieving her goal, and she was for a short time. The problem was, she was too exhausted and teetering on the edge of burnout to savor it. With all Heather's success came more requests, and in turn, more yeses from Heather. She was competent, which meant everyone wanted Heather to do it, take care of it, or speak as an expert about it. Over the course of three years, Heather's role grew from being a lawyer with beloved clients to adding on branch management, systems standardization, people management, and firm-wide complex business law expertise. She not only wore the hats of five people but she was also the only person in her office who knew how to rehab the printer when it jammed, handle escalated client questions, deal with personnel issues, or plan office events.

Home provided Heather no place to rest, which included her husband and three kids. Her three active kids' activities included dance, basketball, soccer, friends, and so many clubs. Her schedule was packed with children's activities and shuttling. She also had about an hour of kids' homework each night because the kids preferred her help over their dad's. The kids always had homework because she and her husband expected As.

After tackling kid homework and dinner duties, she'd log back on to work to answer time-sensitive client questions. Because of this, Heather's husband often felt ignored. Heather hadn't taken a real vacation in years. Due to the weight of her daily client duties and the escalated leadership roles she was stretched to play, she was pulled in all directions and a vacation day wasn't one of them. She told me, "I work Saturday and Sunday just so I can take off Monday." While she wanted to hire people to help, she admitted it took so long to train them and develop the necessary expertise that she found it faster to just do it herself.

As if all of this wasn't enough, she posted on social media as the end of the school year approached, "Anyone else panicking about getting end-of-year teacher gifts done?" She was curious if she was alone in frantically writing notes and arranging gifts for each of her three kids' teachers. Having never given teacher gifts myself, I messaged her to ask, "Is this a new thing?" She responded and let me know that in her circles it was a thing— especially given how hard teachers work lately in the pandemic era. She told me that she was stressed because she still had more "real work" to do when she was done with gifts, and it was going to be a long night.

THE UNPAID WORKLOAD OF WOMEN

Heather was stuck and suffering in the battle that keeps women labeled "unstrategic" and overwhelmed, a phenomenon known as the unpaid workload of women. She was too exhausted and burned out to even know where to begin on setting boundaries so she could do less, reclaim her energy, and level up her role as a confident leader. The unpaid workload of women reveals that women spend an extra two hours per day outside their normal shift at work, cleaning, carpooling, cooking, laundering, parenting, helping family, and more. They are the extra things women say yes to that aren't actually paid, but they are contributing to society and taking our time, our energy, and our effort.

In addition to the two hours of unpaid labor women take on at home, *Harvard Business Review* published that women get 44 percent more requests at work to volunteer for "nonpromotable" tasks at work. Nonpromotable tasks are those that benefit the organization but likely don't contribute to someone's performance evaluation and career advancement. These tasks include traditional office "housework," such as coordinating parties and office events, as well as filling in for a colleague, taking notes, or serving on low-level committees. For Heather, it also included changing all the printer cartridges or holding sole knowledge of the office filing system. Men will tend to go for more strategic projects with higher-level networking or visibility. According to this research, when the requests for nonpromotable tasks occur and decision time comes, 51 percent of the time men said yes, and 76 percent of the time women said yes.

The toll of this unpaid work has real, hard costs. According to the 2021 Women in the Workplace Report by McKinsey, women are contributing more, yet they are often less recognized. Burnout is at an all-time high. While women were resilient during the COVID-19 pandemic response by leading the emotional response and diversity and inclusion efforts, the report revealed that four in ten women had considered leaving their company or switching jobs—and the turnover data in the months following this report indicates they followed through.

This is not just a social justice nor a simple equality issue. Equal pay for labor is an economic issue. It is also not a men-versus-women issue, as men are putting in the work. According to Oxfam, women of all ages and races, income brackets, and employment statuses are spending over 37 percent more time on unpaid labor than men. Paying for these tasks benefits everyone—families, employers, and communities—especially people of color, who experience a far wider pay gap. The Council for Foreign Relations did a study demonstrating that if women had parity with men in terms of paid labor, it would add a GDP gain of $4.3 trillion. That's $13,392 per person—seems worth taking a look at the unpaid labor at work and home.

Organizations need to continue waking up to evaluating the policies they have to keep women and working moms in the office, including equitable distribution of unpaid office work and volunteer opportunities. Women also have permission *not* to be the person that's constantly rushing in and volunteering to save the day at home or work. I see many self-identified strong women busy keeping their careers humming, while navigating the pandemic, contributing to company growth, and climbing the career ladder—often while having families. This is amazing, but know that being a strong and empowered woman doesn't mean you also have to be everything to everyone or the person who always says yes. In fact, as you accelerate in your career, saying yes to too many things will keep you stuck in the weeds, not leading at the strategic level you are capable of.

For women, this is dangerous, as *Harvard Business Review* has reported that women get less specific performance feedback than men, including being told they're not strategic enough and being passed over for promotions given to men. This is where leadership support systems need to be checked. Has a woman leader been given the development resources to succeed? Is she continually presented with nonstrategic projects and then told she's not strategic?

For Heather, and all women who are feeling crushed under the unpaid workload, it's not about hustling to be seen or hoping someone will recognize our efforts. There is still no award for how much you can tolerate. No amount of pay will make up for misery if you are burned out and exhausted. For leaders who are looking to find relief from this workload and be capable of delegating more work to their team, it's time to build women's confidence and lead more by doing *less*.

As I, and the clients I work with, rose throughout the ranks, we were continually presented with opportunities to do more. It's enticing to do more, as we often believe that hustling and saying yes to everything is what will get us noticed. For a while, it works beautifully . . . until we crash and burn. As a woman leader, notice what types of projects you're saying yes to. How strategic are they? Are they aligned with your talents and values? Do they promote your visibility, or are they just keeping you busy? You don't need to settle for less than you deserve. Men won't. You can be a leader who owns her space and delegates and develops others like a pro. This is important because basic delegation skills in your daily work are only half the battle. It's important to master your time and energetic boundaries. In doing this, you will cultivate the ability to lead more by doing less, even as the patriarchal systems of work push against your efforts every day—especially for women leaders. It's hard to build sustainable confidence if you're consistently overworked and overwhelmed.

DO L.E.S.S.

Our culture doesn't fancy up any talk of doing less. In the Western world, we don't tweet or post about sitting still. We post about awards, busyness, accomplishments, and being out and about with our friends. The normal post on your newsfeed isn't "couch surfed all weekend . . . felt great!" We don't scroll stop on people bragging about how they delegated out 50 percent of their meetings that week. But maybe we should.

In a world that glamorizes hustle, packed schedules, and saying yes to *all the things*, there is little room for talk about doing less. In fact, when I bring up this concept for the first time with my clients, they are *not* convinced. After we get clear on values, unique skills, and talents, the next thing I work on is doing *less*. Why? Because unless you unload all the extra workload, shoulds, commitments, and hustle, it's hard to move forward. Ever tried to carry a suitcase without wheels across an airport? It sucks, you have to keep switching arms, and by the time you reach the gate, you're sore and exhausted. You haven't even departed for your destination, and you're already crushing under the weight.

The resistance to doing less is not surprising when much of our identity is wrapped up in our work. When we meet someone new, it doesn't take long for most people to ask them, "So what do you do?" For high-achieving women, their work, families, and responsibilities define much of who they are, so it's easy to fall into the trap—like I did—of "what I do is who I am." Thus, if I'm not doing *all the things*, then who am I? Just because you are committed to doing *less* doesn't make you less of a woman. Your busy calendar is not a source of true confidence.

DO L.E.S.S.

(L) Lose the limiting belief of why you must say yes when you want to say no.

(E) Express your expectations and communicate boundaries.

(S) Shift your identity from doer to leader.

(S) Start delegating with low-stakes tasks.

All the concepts we've covered so far in this book—claiming your values, being yourself, and owning your unique talents—are critical to building your confidence. They're also the basis for using good discernment on when and how to say yes to the right advancement opportunities. To truly move forward with ease, you first have to leave behind the things that are weighing you down and no longer serve you. It's time to do less by losing some LBs, and by LBs, I mean limiting beliefs.

(L)ose the Limiting Beliefs

Ever notice how quickly your inner talk track jumps in to make you feel guilty about saying no? Pursuing the *right* commitments starts with reflecting why we believe we need to say yes when we want to say no (or vice versa). In my own experiences, and over my years of coaching and training clients to set boundaries, I've noticed that are four common limiting beliefs—inner talk tracks—that convince us to say yes when we really want to say no. Which one(s) sounds like you?

- **Achiever Mindset.** "If say no, people will think I'm not capable. Or they'll think I'm not a high achiever, or worthy of what I've been hired to do."
- **People-Pleasing Mindset.** "If I say no, people will be unhappy with me. Or I'll make them angry."
- **Responsibility/Caretaker Mindset.** "If I say no, people will think I don't support them. Or that I don't care about them."
- **Perfectionist/Risk-Averse Mindset.** "I'll say yes so you can see me as perfect, but I'll procrastinate on delivery until the 'thing' is perfect." On the other side of the coin, it can look like saying no too often because of the thought "I'm not going to say yes until it's perfect or risk-free."

Note the LB above that keeps you saying yes most often and ask yourself, "Is this thought even true? Could the opposite of this thought actually be *more true*?"

Here's how our inner critic likes to play us a bit—I am derailed most often by the achiever mindset. I frequently have said yes to things I should have said no to, but I was concerned people might question my capability. But when I start saying yes to too many things, my plate becomes overfilled. When my plate becomes overfilled, I am scrambling to get everything done. I get tired and miss things. All this extra work I said yes to avoid looking incapable has actually now rendered me incapable, and my burden puts me at risk of delivering subpar work. Delivering subpar work will affect how capable others view me. So it could actually be *more true that* "When I say *no*, people will still think I'm capable." When you say no to the wrong things, your plate stays balanced to work on the right things, with the right energy to deliver the right outcomes. you can repeat this exercise with each of the beliefs above and challenge your thinking behind why you are saying yes. Refer back to chapter two to reframe and practice a more freeing thought track with these limiting beliefs.

(E) xpress Expectations

In order to clear their plate and help others help them, women must get comfortable asking for help, clearly expressing their needs and desired outcomes, and having clear conversations about what they will and will not own. It's not just as easy as saying yes or no. Every conversation you have is teaching people how to use you, what you will tolerate, and what you won't. You have the opportunity in every conversation to set the tone for leadership, for the team, and for yourself.

Telling people what you expect has two steps. Step one is to be clear about what you want and need from people so they don't have to guess. Ambiguity is a big source of animosity between people, and on teams, so success loves clarity in communicating goals, roles, processes, purpose, and desired outcomes. Why do you have to be so clear about expressing what you need and expect from people? We tend to subconsciously believe that what we want and need is "obvious" if we sit in the same meetings together and hear the same strategy updates. Shouldn't they "just know" what outcomes you want? It bears repeating that people are horrible guessers and struggle to read minds.

Imagine this: If I asked you to plan an employee party and hire an Easter Bunny, what type of Easter Bunny would you bring, based on your experiences? A white one? Pink? Gray? Purple? How tall would that Easter Bunny be? Four feet? Six feet? A small one, the size of an actual bunny? If I as your leader was expecting a six-foot-tall and pink Easter Bunny, and you, based on your experiences, delivered up a five-foot-tall and white Easter Bunny, I'm going to feel disappointed. I might start to tell myself a story that you don't listen or understand. You, as my employee, might not understand why I am so frustrated or why I can't be a clear communicator.

While you might be rolling your eyes because I'm talking about a big bunny that delights kids with eggs and candy, this is a symbol of how a lack of shared experiences and understanding manifests into miscommunication and disappointment. In theory, many people know what the Easter Bunny is, but depending on the books we've read, the parties we've attended, or families we grew up in, we may envision it differently. For some people, the Easter Bunny wasn't part of their culture, so it's hard to imagine. This is similar to your team at work—they've all been trained up into the workforce by different leaders, different teachers, taught by different systems or tools. Some of our team is new. Some team members are still acclimating to the culture. Because of all these different experiences, they may imagine a different final outcome than you, even if you share the same idea in theory.

I shared this example with a group of nurse leaders once during a leadership training as a way to create clarity through shared communication and purpose. Admittedly, they thought this Easter Bunny example was a little nuts and didn't find me all that funny in the moment. Then, about one month later, I had a check-in call with one of the nurse leaders, and she excitedly told me, "You know that Easter Bunny exercise you had us do in the group where we had to imagine it, and it was all different? Well, I didn't think we'd need it much. Then we were sitting in a team leader meeting this week, and we were arguing about a policy and desired outcome. A light bulb went on for me that we were all misunderstanding each other. I said to the rest of the group, '*I think we're all talking about different Easter Bunnies here!*'" She told me the tension in the room broke, and everyone laughed. They each went around the table and clearly articulated what they *thought* the desired outcome was, only to learn that many of the leaders had a slightly different take. Once they were able to clearly define and share the vision of the goal and desired outcome, they were able to move forward as a team on delegating out the right next steps.

It bears repeating: success loves clarity. When it comes to delegating work, both paid and unpaid, be clear about the task and outcomes so you don't keep getting pulled back in. To be clear about your expectations, communicate the four Ps:

Purpose: Why are we doing this? Why do I want it? Why does this matter?

People: Who is involved? Who are the decision-makers? Who carries out the work? What roles will each person play in getting the work done?

Process: What work needs to be done by when? What are the steps and timelines involved? How is the work expected to be done?

Performance: What is the ultimate goal? What does success look like?

Part two of expressing your expectations means having a clear boundary conversation framework so you can redistribute and delegate work that is not yours to own. After checking limiting beliefs and getting clear on your best yes (or no), you might wonder, "Well, how do I say this kindly and collaboratively and not sound like a jerk?" Here's a simple boundary-setting process I mastered during my years of leading training teams. Many business issues were labeled a "training issue" no matter what the root cause was, so as the leader of the training department, I had to get skilled up at discerning what was a true training issue versus what was a deeper problem that was trying to use training as a Band-Aid. Also, I had to manage my and my team's workload.

Collaborative and Confident Boundary Conversations

1. Thank them for the ask you're happy to do.
2. Communicate your values and commitments.
3. Describe what you can't accommodate.
4. Turn 1–3 into a question statement.

Here's an example. *"Kelli, can your team do a sales training workshop for us on Tuesday in our all-hands meeting?"* (It's Friday).

Sample answer: *"Thanks for reaching out. I'd be happy to do a workshop (1)! I want to ensure it's relevant and high energy (2), and that typically takes at least two weeks to prepare. Since Tuesday won't provide enough development time (3), how does XX date work for you and your team(4)?"*

I may have offered to come to their all-hands meeting to gather more insight or provide a teaser, but I kept firm on the final commitment. Using this framework opens the door for you to offer help by recommending another person or organization who might be a better partner for them. In that case, it might sound like, *"Thanks for coming to me first! My team doesn't offer the expertise you're looking for / My team is fully focused on their strategic commitments this quarter and is fully booked up. I'd be happy to spend a few minutes brainstorming about who can best help you."*

The keys to saying no with grace are gratitude and collaboration. You are worth the effort of communicating what boundaries you can work within and what you can't accommodate. Remember: only the *wrong* people are angered by your expression of healthy expectations and boundaries.

> You can't expect new results if you won't express your true expectations.

S hift Your Identity from Doer to Leader

The initial acts of delegating all this work can create an identity crisis. In the first half of our life, we are rewarded for our individual contributions. Many of us are told we are great fixers, we're smart, and we generate creative ideas. For me personally, I was often commended for my high level of responsibility to take on and complete tasks. Most of my efforts built an identity that I was the doer, the creative, the responsible one. Our ego loves to build its empire on that identity.

Hoarding tasks that should be let go of often are small, like loading the dishwasher. I open it up to see that my husband or daughter has put the cups where the dishes go and vice versa. Instead of showing them the proper way to load the dishwasher, I open it, moan about it to them while they watch TV, and go about fixing it myself. This only happens once a week. At work, it would start with an honest delegation of what I thought would be a simple project, pulling together a PowerPoint presentation, only to receive it and correct every single slide because it wasn't displayed the way *I* liked it.

What we tend to do as leaders, and as parents or partners, when things aren't done the way we prefer to do them, is to step in with frustration and give our ego the fix it's learned to enjoy from our individual doer days. We "save the day" by taking over the task and reworking it to the way we like it. It just feels better, faster, and easier that way. While our intentions are to be helpful, what tends to happen is we inadvertently breed a bit of learned helplessness—the people around us assume the belief they aren't capable of doing the task on their own. The team working for us, or our partner or children, often throw up their hands: "Why should I even try to complete this project (or load the dishwasher) because my boss is just going to come and fix and redo my work." Over time, when work is continually erased and redone, employee confidence wanes, and the drive to give good effort is diminished.

As the leader delegating, it creates an exhausting fix/overwhelm cycle. We think, "I just want to take this project back because I want things done my way. Nobody else does things as well or as fast as I can." Thus, leaders do all the things until they also throw up their hands in frustration and overwhelm, saying, "Why am I the only one who does anything around here?"

As leaders, we have to make the shift from doer and fixer to leader and coach. We can't have it both ways. We can choose be the one who does everything and enjoys rewards as an individual contributor, or we can learn to delegate and embrace the rewards that come from coaching people through the learning process. Yes, teaching and learning is slower, and it requires more patience.

I know how hard this is to watch someone struggle through an effort. I don't know if it's more painful for them as the learner or me as the watcher.

Self-reflection is a good place to begin shifting our identity from doer to leader at work by reflecting on the best leader you had in your career. My sense is that this leader is not someone who hoarded work and spent their hours unraveling your efforts and redoing your tasks. My guess is that it's probably someone who delegated challenging projects to you, even those that felt a tad out of reach, and then allowed you to complete those projects, albeit with a few mistakes. And with these mistakes, they likely turned those into learning moments, with plenty of coaching through the process. All the struggle didn't hurt you; it likely built your confidence muscles for bigger future projects.

When it comes to reducing the workload that's causing burnout, it will be hard to make true changes unless we first make a mindset and identify shift and recognize that a great leader feels satisfied not by saving the day herself but by having a strong team she's built to make the save.

(S) tart Delegating

Many leaders tell me they can't delegate because people seem to make high-impact mistakes. This is true when we wait to delegate tasks when the stakes are high. If we reflect back on our leader Heather, this was a big cause of concern for her. She was holding on to everything like glue because shifting your mindset around delegating is hard work. Then her unmanageable workload would force her to delegate—often in high-stakes moments when the tolerance for mistakes is low. This creates a chaotic scenario in which the tension is already high, and we are expecting big things from a team member who may have little to no experience delivering on such a high-profile project.

The key here is to start delegating when the stakes are *low*. We have a higher tolerance for making mistakes in low-stakes situations. So, if you're looking to develop someone's presentation skills, what low-risk environments can you place an individual in while they gain comfort in building up their skills so they can make mistakes safely? Then, when they are called to the table when the stakes are high, they have confident repetitions under their belt. Are you working on an activity or project that is no longer a development opportunity for you? Delegate it. Someone on your team is hoping for opportunities to grow, and these make perfect circumstances to do so. Let's see this in action.

DELEGATING DEVELOPS CONFIDENCE

"I'd love to work on building my executive presentation skills," I said to my manager, Valerie.

"Oh, awesome. You know how I have you prepare your business unit presentation deck so I can present it to the C-Suite every month? Plan on presenting it yourself next month."

My stomach flipped, and my face got warm. I wanted to work on my executive presentation skills to build my confidence, but I didn't expect to go straight to the top to practice. Self-doubt crept in, but I knew I'd have a couple of weeks to calm my nerves and pull my presentation together. I was a director at a regional bank, leading a training and development team, as well as a financial education team who sold our branch banking products to business clients in our market. I worked to pull in our monthly numbers, but this time with extra scrutiny because I would be the one doing the talking in front of a more senior audience.

I gathered our training results, customer experience scores, and sales results. I projected our revenue and expenses for the next quarter. The CEO also wanted my projections for the next year, along with justifications behind my sales and expenses. He was a newer CEO, a well-known leader from the megabanks, who had come to help our regional bank turn some financial corners during the banking crisis of 2008. He was friendly and disarming in talking with him personally, but he took no fluff in meetings. He became known for demanding your stretch goals to be your new minimum standards. I prepared my deck, reviewed it with Valerie, and took the long ride up the elevator to the thirty-ninth floor. I was nervous and pitting out in my Ann Taylor suit, but ready.

Or so I thought.

In the room that day was the CEO of the bank, my boss, Valerie, the head of our retail banking division (her boss), the CFO, and me. I started in on my presentation, and the first five minutes were off and running. *I'm doing well,* was my initial thought. Then the CEO started rapid-firing his questions, especially related to the financial education business development team I led. "How did you arrive at this number? Can't you do better? Isn't there a wider market than this? Why do you think this is a valuable product for us?" I could feel my face and neck glow bright red. I was starting to stutter in my answers a bit. Quite frankly, he was asking some questions I didn't have ready answers to. I felt like I was observing my own train wreck in action.

Then the dagger. He looked at my other two bosses. "Should we even keep offering this service to our clients?" They both smiled and said something appropriate, I am sure. I can't remember what save they offered at that time, because I was so anxiety-ridden and overwhelmed. I don't know who felt the most pain in that meeting, me, with the hot neck and sweaty armpits, or my boss, Valerie, who was watching the train wreck go down in real time. I have observed my own share of meeting bombs, and they are not easy to watch.

But she didn't intervene. She let me carry on with my presentation, let me handle the answers, and only answered when the CEO directed questions at her. When the meeting closed, we walked into the elevator and started the ride down thirty-nine floors. She turned to me and smiled. "So, how do you think that went?"

I unloaded. "Oh my God, I did horrible! He asked all sorts of questions I wasn't prepared for, and I stuttered like an idiot. I can't believe I did that. I'm a mess, and that did *not* go as I planned."

She was calm and replied, "I noticed that too. We've all had our first presentation to executives, and I know many people say they wish it went differently. What do you think you can do next time to make it go more smoothly?"

Next time? What? But I replied, "I'm not sure; I'll give it some thought." She agreed this was a good idea and asked that I bring my reflections to our next one-to-one meeting.

You might be thinking Valerie is a horrible leader for letting me commit a slow form of career death in that meeting. But what if this type of leadership is exactly what women need to lead more confidently, develop others, and cultivate their teams so they can *do less?* Valerie knew exactly what she was doing. I asked her for an opportunity to build my executive presence and presentation skills, and she delivered. She prepped her boss, who was the head of retail banking, the CFO, and the CEO that I would be coming in that day to present because it was a stretch assignment I desired. Honestly, I think the CEO was having a little bit of fun peppering a young director. It helped my ego stay in check.

In contrast, they were providing me a perfect example of delegating a career growth opportunity when the stakes are *low*. Everyone knew this was my first time. She gave me the authority to prepare and present my work. They all gave me grace for the mistakes they knew I would make. In our later meetings, Valerie asked me helpful questions so I could self-reflect on my experience and opportunities for growth, with questions like: *Who do you know that always seems to present well to senior leaders? Who do you admire for their abilities to present the numbers? How can you find their approaches and weave them into your own style?* I was able to incorporate these approaches and slowly get better each time I presented in front of leadership. To this day, I ask myself these questions every time I speak in public so I can always be sharpening my skills. It was a gift of a lifelong lesson.

Many leaders, at the request of one of their team members, may have reacted in one of two ways. First, they may have not given their team member such a visible way to test their skills. Second, at the first sign of things going south, they might have rushed in to save the day and save face and taken over the presentation. If I'm being honest, up until that point in my career, I was the latter. I had been in my own meetings and seen my team members struggle, only felt the pain myself, and stepped in to take over. But the act of taking over isn't helpful it all; it's actually harmful to the confidence of the employee and development of the team. When people learn they don't have to fully prepare, and that their boss will save them every time they stumble, they learn to only prepare the bare minimum.

This hurts the employee because they never grow their capability and confidence because the leader is taking over just at the moment of struggle, which is where the learning happens. (I do this as a parent too.) This hurts the leader because they are always stepping in to save the day and can start believing they are the only one capable of doing anything. They start to believe they can't count on anyone. This leads them to say yes to more, rescue others more during valuable learning opportunities, hustle more, and eventually burn out more. Two people lose confidence in this scenario: the leader and the employee.

PRACTICE CLARITY, AUTHORITY, AND GRACE

In addition to delegating tasks and projects while the stakes are low, there are three practices to embrace to help you delegate like a pro. First, practice *clarity*. While I covered this earlier in the chapter, ensure you have been crystal clear about what is expected in the ask. What are the purposes, people roles, process steps, and performance outcomes you expect? (Be sure you're talking about the same Easter Bunny here.)

Second, practice giving *authority*. When you delegate a meeting or leadership in a project, ensure that the other stakeholders know that you've crowned your team member as decision-maker, and they should go directly to that individual. The ownership and accountability of delegation is negated when everyone is still coming to you for the updates, decisions, and answers.

Finally, practice giving *grace*. Grace doesn't mean you tolerate poor effort or careless mistakes. Grace is offering kindness and accommodation in the face of someone not doing something *exactly how you would do it.* Giving grace is offering gentle yet direct feedback on how someone can improve their delivery in their own way, using their best talents, even if it's not *your way.* Practicing grace allows someone a safe place to make mistakes because they are human and learning. Grace is essential, because if a leader doesn't create a safe space for people to make earnest mistakes while learning the ropes, she will find herself with a team who is unwilling to try anything new. Wondering how to say all this? There is a framework to help you give feedback in your authentic style in the "Amplify Your Voice" chapter.

DUMP, DELEGATE, AND OUTSOURCE

Rest. Self-care. Anti-hustle. These might feel like dirty words in corporate America today. I'm ready to challenge a culture that we buy into—a belief that feeling overworked and riding the edge of burnout means we are doing great work. I'm tired of tolerating this belief that if we're not suffering a little bit under the weight of a packed schedule, then we aren't working hard enough. If we want to keep women, especially working mothers, in the work-force, it's time to find more sanity in our schedules. Every quarter, I encourage my clients to do a calendar audit and determine what they can dump, delegate, and outsource so they can find a better work-life rhythm.

DUMP IT

It happens to all of us—things that we said yes to months or years ago that we keep doing because we're on autopilot. In my own experience, these were old reports I would review that no one was paying attention to. They were meetings I was still attending because I was invited once and kept going, even though I could just be informed after the meeting. These also can include yeses you once said to a friend group or to your child's school that no longer align with your values. Look at your calendar and task list. You have permission to dump it because it drains you.

Ask yourself: Do I need or want to be there? Does this align with my values, talents, or priorities?

DELEGATE IT

If you can't dump it, can you delegate it? In a day of back-to-back meetings, I noticed that two of my team members were in there with me. They could handle the meeting and make the decisions, but because I was in the meeting as their leader, people would defer to me anyhow. My presence in the room was actually *hindering* their development. I decided to delegate that meeting and every other meeting like it. The newfound white space on my calendar freed me up to pursue more strategic priorities. At home, when I was a working single mom, my daughter was taught to do her laundry from the time she could reach the knobs. It was a great life skill for her. So was cleaning the bathroom. She did a terrible job at first, but I have to admit she has some pretty high standards for cleanliness now as a teenager.

Ask yourself: Does my presence add or subtract value for fellow team members also in the meeting? Is this a development opportunity for my team to lead? How many salary dollars are sitting here? Are we getting a positive return for them? At home, ask yourself what chores you can delegate to your kids, or even a neighbor's child who wants to build their skills.

OUTSOURCE IT

If you can't dump it or delegate it, can you outsource it? In my years of working at technology and consulting firms, I discovered the power of outsourcing. We had small but mighty teams. So there weren't layers of hierarchy that could handle lots of delegation assignments; however, we owned the power of contractors. We outsourced everything from office grocery and snack delivery—yes, we used to have a full-time person spend their precious hours doing this—to our printing needs. We found reliable people to outsource marketing activities that we couldn't handle.

As a working mom, I outsourced my lawn care and snow removal to neighbors. When I got remarried, my husband gladly took that over, but I have a confession to make: My daughter had a summer job at age fifteen, and some days we had to outsource her ride to work. Yep, I called her an Uber. My husband and I, even though we worked from home, were busy with clients. We could have tried to reschedule our day and hustle to make the twenty-five-minute round trip commute, or we could hire a professional. So we did. She thought it was cool to have a "driver," and I tracked her the whole way while keeping my clients on schedule. Win-win.

Ask yourself: Is this mine to own? Is this adding to my stress and unpaid workload? Can someone do it better and faster than me? What can be outsourced to a professional that will save time, sanity, and overwork—and maybe even money in the long run?

CLOSE THE CONFIDENCE GAP TOOL KIT

LEAD MORE BY DOING LESS

NOTICE IT

Where is my unpaid workload showing up at work or home? (Hint: notice where you feel resentful of the task or envious of others who opted out.)

OWN IT (OR NOT)

What is truly mine to own here (tasks, projects, responsibilities, etc.)?

- Am I self-imposing my obligations or deadlines?
- What is not mine to own?

REFRAME IT

DO L.E.S.S.

(L) Lose the limiting belief of why you must say yes when you want to say no.

What is a truer belief that helps me advance with confidence?

ACT ON IT

Boost your peace, your potential, and your paycheck by setting your boundaries, delegating what drains you, and clearing your calendar to empower your clear and confident leadership.

(E) Express your expectations and communicate boundaries.

(S) Shift your identity from doer to leader.

(S) Start delegating with low-stakes tasks.

Calendar detox: *Take a look at your calendar in the next thirty to ninety days. Look at your professional and personal meetings, project requests, or task list. Reflect on your values, your talents, and your unique skills; are your commitments in alignment with them? Then ask yourself what you can dump, delegate, or outsource.*

Visit CLOSINGTHECONFIDENCEGAP.COM/BOOKDOWNLOADS for a printable version of this tool or the entire workbook of tools in this book.

6

TRUST YOURSELF

Learning to trust your instincts, using your intuitive sense of
what's best for you, is paramount to any lasting success. I've
trusted the still, small voice of my intuition my entire life. And
the only time I've made mistakes is when I didn't listen.

OPRAH WINFREY

n my midthirties, I had to make one of the hardest decisions of
my life. Ignoring everyone's guidance that I should stay single
for a while after my divorce from my first husband, I hopped
right back in and started a new relationship. We dated for
about five years and were engaged for just over one year of that
time. About eight months from the wedding, I started to have
doubts, but moments of fun or laughter would bring back my
optimism. The highs were fun and likely appeared perfect from
the outside, but lows came suddenly and often left me feeling
crazy and confused. As we approached four months out from the
wedding, I was silently wrestling with serious indecision about
staying in the relationship.

I spent endless nights crawling the internet, entering search phrases such as "How do you know if they're the one?" "How do you call off a wedding?" "What is the difference between cold feet and just nerves?" "What's normal fiancé behavior in wedding planning?" I felt a craving to be absolutely certain about my decision. If I made the choice to call off the wedding and end the relationship, I knew it would not just be about me—it would have a massive ripple effect throughout family and friends.

Desperate for the right answer, I journaled as much as I could about the situation, hoping that seeing things on paper and looking at my future through the lens of pros and cons might bring the aha moment I craved. On paper, there were things that looked great, and there continued to be some red flags, but I rationalized them, citing that no one was perfect. I felt a strange fear of failure in that this could be my second long-term relationship that failed. The achiever part of me wanted it to succeed, and I wondered if something was wrong with me. So, when neither the internet nor my writing was delivering up certainty in answers, I started asking people I trusted. I talked to my parents, my siblings, and my closest friends. I talked with my therapist. Everyone was supportive of me in my indecision yet gracefully held back their true opinions so I could make the right choice for me.

The stress of the indecision and pending wedding date was taking a toll on my body. I started feeling pain on the left side of my stomach that was so persistent my doctor recommended an ultrasound to see if there was an intestinal issue. When the scans came up clear, it was my massage therapist who discovered that my psoas muscle in my stomach was so tight from sitting crunched and clenched from stress every day.

I had to find relief. I had to find clarity.

One day one of my colleagues, Denise, came in for our one-on-one meeting. We'd developed a strong relationship, and she was familiar with my situation. I think she could see I was stressed, and she asked how things were going. I told her about everything I was doing to solve my dilemma—all the internet searches, the worry, the journaling, the couples therapy, the input from my family. I shared again my concerns for the future about proceeding with the wedding. I teared up while picking apart my anxieties about the difference between having cold feet and something being a wrong decision. I thought out loud that maybe just time or more couples therapy or maybe more effort on my end would fix the issues that needed to be resolved for me to feel comfortable to proceed with the wedding—I didn't know what to do, but something wasn't feeling right.

Denise softly looked at me in the eyes and delivered a gem of wisdom I've come to know her for. "God [the Universe, Creator] is not the author of chaos. She is the author of peace. She never intended you to live a life of chaos. You will know what to do because the right decision will always feel peaceful."

Her words, the thought that I was meant to feel peace, sent tingles up my spine. My shoulders dropped, and my stomach expanded with relief. I felt twenty pounds lighter. In that moment, it was as if my gut, my heart, and my head connected all the dots five years backward, and my decision, albeit terrifying, felt clear as a bell. I knew exactly what I needed to do. I didn't have certainty on how this would all pan out in the end, but I felt instant clarity—I knew what peace felt like in my body, and I wanted my future to be full of it. I had to call off the wedding.

I could barely utter those words aloud because I felt like a huge failure—a divorce and now this? I was convinced my "picker" was broken. This is where I had to stand firm in trusting my gut, owning my peace, and holding the confidence of choosing myself. I learned that my gut is going to tell me things that my mind, my ego, is *not* going to like. It will ask me to make hard decisions that might disappoint people. This is why it's so important to claim your values, own your talents, and hold a confident mindset, because sometimes your gut is going to nudge you in a way that might shatter everything you thought you knew. I don't know about you, but my gut is never wrong.

A few weeks later, I summoned the words and the courage to hold one of the hardest conversations of my life and told him I couldn't move forward with the wedding and wanted to end the relationship. Just because you know you've made the right decision, it doesn't make carrying out that decision easy. Disappointing people is hard, but I learned that disappointing myself, especially my future self, would turn out to be even harder. At the end of the day, I knew I had to trust myself.

In the months that followed my wedding call-off, I did the hard work of identifying and living by my values. I set boundaries in my work and personal lives and made difficult, albeit liberating choices in alignment with them. Sometimes I wondered if I set my standards too high when I felt lonely. But the solitude was healing and necessary for coming back to who I really was and what I truly wanted; however, I was happy in so many ways I'd never experienced before and grateful I trusted myself.

About seven months after I ended the engagement, my boss started to ask me if I was dating again, to which I emphatically told her no—I thought that the dating pool for women my age (thirty-six at the time) was contaminated. She lovingly encouraged me to consider online dating, as that's how she met her husband, and rattled off many examples of other women who did the same. I wasn't convinced, so she made a bet with me that late October afternoon. She said if I wasn't dating anyone by New Year's Day, then I would need to fill out my online dating profile. I gave her a half-hearted "Okay, fine," thinking she would conveniently forget.

Well, New Year's Eve came, and my date canceled a few hours before our plans started, so I spent New Year's Eve as a third wheel with another couple. I was still not planning on completing my Match.com profile on January 1, until I got a call from my sister, who was also single. She said, "So I've been thinking of joining Match . . . " I found this all too serendipitous, so I came clean about the bet I had made with my boss that I conveniently just lost. So the joke ended up being on me while we giggled with a glass of wine, trying to answer the online profile questions in the most flattering way. While an initial crap show of cheesy pickup lines commenced in my Match message box, tempting me to delete the app, I came across a picture of a guy with scroll-stopping ocean-blue eyes. I was too scared to message him, so I simply clicked *like* on his photo. He messaged me back with quite the original pickup line: "Hey, how are ya."

As we began talking, we found uncanny similarities, from attending the same high school to sharing a similar friend circle. He even worked as a financial advisor alongside my mother for a few years. We'd been passing by one another for decades, and we didn't even know it. As we began dating, it was easy because we shared so many of the same values that allowed us to do life together in the same way. I didn't just feel physically safe with him but emotionally safe. Around him, I never had to pretend, hide, or walk on eggshells. I could always be myself. He loved me "flaws" and all and saw them as my gifts. He supported me and my daughter unconditionally in our goals. He's now my husband.

Marrying him always felt of peace.

WHAT THEY DON'T TEACH YOU IN LEADERSHIP PROGRAMS

My point in telling you such a personal story in a confidence and leadership book is that we tend to overuse our head, logic, and analytical skills to lead our lives and make our decisions. It's no wonder that we head down the wrong path, follow the "rules," trip up on our decisions, or fall into analysis paralysis—talking ourselves into decisions that appear right on paper but leave us unsettled in our body.

I designed, developed, and facilitated leadership development programs in organizations for years. I earned my MBA and then taught management courses at the university level. I sat in several excellent leadership development programs. Most of what is taught is what I now refer to as *neck up* leadership development. They teach you how to analyze a profit and loss sheet, how to use strategic planning, how to give feedback, how to follow a performance management process, and so on. They provide lists and characteristics of what is said to be an ideal leadership style or successful executive presence, much of which is based on a historically masculine leadership approach. All these tools, strategies, and processes are helpful, but they're missing a huge chunk of our intelligence from the *neck down*—our heart and gut.

Many successful leaders tell me that they use all the good, analytical leadership and strategy tools taught in leadership programs and books, but when the time comes to make a difficult decision, they often rely on their gut. What I believe is missing from the leadership programs of the future is learning to go neck down and use your head *and* heart *and* gut to make the right decisions for you, your teams, and the organization. This is why I've encouraged you to listen to your body when claiming your values and to notice if your energy drains or surges in response to your work. What I teach my clients and in my leadership programs, and what I'll show you how to do in the sections that follow, is how to *trust yourself* as a leader—how to cut through all the chaos, the data, the analysis paralysis, the opinions of others, and gain clarity on the right choice for you.

The world is noisy with so much available advice on social media, in books, and leadership articles. There is no shortage of opinions on how you should lead and the actions you should take, so trusting yourself is more important than ever today. There are daily challenges to listening to our heart and gut, which people often describe as their intuition. Intuition isn't a "woo-woo" experience accessed through lighting candles or meditation; many people describe it as a knowing or a "gut feeling." Hence, people frequently use the terms *gut* and *intuition* interchangeably. Gavin de Becker, author of *The Gift of Fear*, describes intuition as "the journey from A to Z without stopping at any other letter along the way. It is knowing without knowing why."

My clients have described it as a little nudge or gentle voice. Ignoring your intuition is very common, especially for women who've spent years working in corporate organizations. We grow accustomed to following a script or organizational rules. We've often overlooked our intuition, hidden our "unlikeable" qualities and true voice, to follow a path that we've been told would make us happy or successful, to get us to the desired office, salary, or title. In our busy (often unpaid) workloads between work and home, many women are too busy or overworked to remember to think about checking in with themselves. How often have you quieted your still, small voice because you were too distracted or took a colleague's advice instead?

I get it. Facts matter. In many organizations the PowerPoint deck, financial statement, or scorecard is king. I grew up in financial services, and in my logical, direct, and sometimes unemotional approach, I overvalued my head over my heart and gut. Data is very important in making decisions, *and* coupled with the power of your intuition, it is your competitive advantage as a leader. You have a powerful tool inside your body that *knows* what's right for *you*. You are equipped with everything you need to use your authentic leadership style to make decisions on your ideal career, relationships, and business goals. Imagine if you knew exactly how to check this inner way of knowing for every important decision in your life—where could this intelligence take you?

YOUR COMPETITIVE ADVANTAGE AS A LEADER

Some of the world's most successful leaders reiterate that trusting their gut is their competitive advantage. Oprah says that your intuition doesn't lie and that trusting her instincts has made all the difference in her career. Steve Jobs says that everything is "secondary" to following your heart and intuition because they already know what you want to become.

Jamie Kern Lima founded IT Cosmetics on her living room floor. Plagued with a skin condition called rosacea and hyperpigmentation, she couldn't find makeup products in the market that looked and felt as she wanted, so she created them herself. She started as a small shop, selling to friends, family, and locally, and eventually online and to trade shows. She knew she'd created something special because her brand of makeup was *not* built for people with perfect skin, and she wanted to reflect that. As her dreams for her makeup brand grew, she recognized that she needed help and capital, so she began seeking out venture capitalists to invest in her company.

She kept hearing denial after denial. Investors kept telling her that while they thought the product was great, she needed to change her marketing approach. Instead of using herself as the primary face and model of the company, they wanted her to use models that one would think of in the beauty industry— tall, perfect eyebrows, flawless skin, high cheekbones, and right around 115 pounds.

Knowing that her company was reaching its last penny and desperate for help, she was tempted to go against her gut and acquiesce to what the investors wanted so that she could make a name for her company and get the resources she needed to survive. As she reflected on the future, one of the approaches in alignment with her values was having real women with real skin problems see themselves in her branding and product demonstrations. She knew if she didn't align with her values, then she would resent the success. Her gut continued to tell her no—do not conform to what the industry has always done, say no to investors who want you to change your values-based approach.

After years of noes and close to broke, she earned a chance to do a ten-minute demonstration of her product on QVC. The amount of product she had to prepurchase in case of a sellout would likely break her company if it didn't work—but Jamie knew she was all in and this was going to be either her big break or going-out-of-business event.

Encouraged and tempted again to use traditional industry models in her QVC demonstration, she chose again to go with her gut and values and use herself—flawed skin and all—as the model. When the makeup artist wiped away the flawless product to reveal Jamie's underlying skin condition, the product sold out in minutes. IT went on to become the largest beauty brand in QVC history, and a few years later, Jamie sold IT Cosmetics for a record-breaking $1.2 billion (yes, billion) to L'Oréal. Now considered one of the richest self-made women, she has frequently attributed her success to "being obsessed" with trusting her gut and not conforming to what others wanted her to be just to be successful.

Let's see how strong the career-intuition connection is for you:

CAREER INTUITION QUIZ

1. Looking back over your career, has the information your intuition (gut) given you been mostly true?

   Usually (3)   Sometimes (2)   Rarely (1)

2. When you get seemingly smart career advice, but it doesn't align with your intuition, do you reject it?

   Usually (3)   Sometimes (2)   Rarely (1)

3. Can you pinpoint the early signals your body gives you when you are overworking or burnt out?

   Usually (3)   Sometimes (2)   Rarely (1)

4. During the course of your career, have you primarily chosen roles based on what lights you up over what appears to be the next logical title or salary step?

   Usually (3)   Sometimes (2)   Rarely (1)

5. When making a big decision at work, do you listen to your intuitive hunches and body responses to guide you to the right choice?

   Usually (3)   Sometimes (2)   Rarely (1)

6. Do you listen to your body's signals and energy levels to set boundaries with people who drain you?

   Usually (3)   Sometimes (2)   Rarely (1)

7. Can you tell the difference between the voice of your intuition and your ego?

   Usually (3)   Sometimes (2)   Rarely (1)

8. Do you often overthink or talk yourself out of a decision your intuition says is right?

   Usually (1)   Sometimes (2)   Rarely (3)

9. Do you know exactly how, and where, your body gives you the signals for a yes or no?

   Usually (3)   Sometimes (2)   Rarely (1)

0–6 Points

It appears that it may be time to reconnect with your body! This is very common, especially for women who've spent years working in corporate organizations or are buried in high workloads. We grow accustomed to following a script or organizational rules. We've often overlooked our intuition and true voice to follow a path that we've been told would make us happy or successful.

7–12 Points

You are getting big clues from your intuition—and sometimes you put them into action! Does that typically work successfully for you? What if you could fully reconnect with your body? Feeling a little disconnected is very common, especially for women who've spent years working in corporate organizations. We grow accustomed to following a script or organizational rules. We've often overlooked our intuition and true voice to follow a path that we've been told would make us happy or successful. How often have you quieted your still, small voice because you believed a colleague's advice instead?

12–18 Points

You are well connected and consistently dialing into your intuition. Are the decisions you make by having confidence in your intuition typically those that work out best for you? What if you could strengthen your intuition even more and feel fully confident in trusting your still, small voice to bring you the clarity you desire in your career and life? How could this create total alignment between your work, your values, and creating the work you are meant to do?

YOUR BODY IS WISER THAN YOUR MIND

Now more than ever, there are algorithms, experts, influencers, friends, videos, and leaders who want to tell you the right thing to do. The world continues to get noisier so you have to learn how to trust yourself. How can you truly slow down, relax, and get still enough to trust your body so you know if your heart and gut, your intuition, is telling you yes or no?

First, let's talk about the science of how your intuition works and how your body is sending yes or no signals to your brain. If this at all feels woo-woo to you, I hear you. Given my background was all corporate financial services and technology, I wanted no part of this "check in with your body" business when I first learned it from Martha Beck (known as Oprah's life coach) in coach training and in her book *Finding Your Own North Star*. After learning some of the data and science behind it, however, I gave in. I'm glad I did because it was one of the most life-changing tools I've ever learned in all my years of personal and professional development. It validated the advice that Denise offered me that day to follow what peace felt like in my body.

Researchers at the University of Iowa wanted to better understand decision-making as it relates to cognition and emotion. Ultimately, the study revealed the science of intuition. One of the main questions taken into this study was: When people are gambling, do they know they're starting to get themselves into some trouble? At what point do they know if things are going well, or going south?

In this experiment, participants are presented with four face-down decks of cards. They can flip over cards from any deck. Most cards earn a reward and some cards create a penalty. In the four decks, some contain more reward-earning cards than others. As the participants pull cards, they should start noticing which decks are best and start flipping cards only from the highest-paying decks. The experiment is believed to measure the emotional part of learning, or intuition, based on reward and punishment of winning cards and penalty cards. It's thought that the participants begin to "feel" which decks are best and worst.

The results were fascinating: Most healthy participants took between forty and fifty card flips to recognize the difference between the winning and losing decks and then stick to the good ones. But skin tests—like those used with lie detectors—showed that after only about ten card flips, the participants started to show stress responses (i.e., perspiration) as their hands hovered above bad decks.

Here's the bottom line that I bet you already knew deep in your gut. It's what I recognized deep in my gut after my conversation with Denise about my wedding—you know when you've got a bad deck before your mind will make sense of it.

Think about it this way. Have you ever felt something in your gut that you just couldn't put into words? Maybe you found yourself trying to describe how you felt about something or someone, but you just couldn't find the right words to say how and what you were feeling in your body about it. There's just this *knowing* without being able to explain why or how.

The science continues to show that you're right—your body *is* wiser than your mind. A fascinating statistic uncovered by cognitive psychologists working to understand the amount of information we perceive is that your verbal brain processes information at about forty bits per second, which sounds rapidly awesome! But these psychologists highlight another fascinating find from neuroscience. Neuroscientists say we actually have three brains—the one in our head, which we tend to overuse in Western society and corporate culture, but there are two more brains—in the heart and in the gut. They make up the cluster of nerves that forms our gut brain, our intuition. It gathers information at *eleven million* bits per second.

So it's your body that's getting more signals than your brain can process, not vice versa like you might be inclined to think. It explains why you get gut feelings on things that you just can't explain or put into words. It's why you struggle to articulate what you "just know." It's why you trust your gut to just check on the baby one more time or to call the doctor for a second opinion. It's why you can look at all the data, the spreadsheet, and the PowerPoint presentation full of facts, consider it, and go with the career or leadership decision that feels right in your gut—and it turns out to be successful for you. Your body knows the difference between dread and freedom, between chaos and peace. It signals to you your heck yes and hell no. It is the foundation of true confidence in yourself.

> A confident woman **trusts herself**; her body is trustworthy.

HOW TO FIND YOUR
HECK YES AND HELL NO

I'm sure you're wrestling with some type of decision right now as you're reading this. It could be a big decision, like changing jobs or calling off a wedding. It could be a small decision, like choosing whether to say yes to a holiday party invite or choosing a project to complete at work. Note a decision that you need to make below; try a small one while you're testing this out.

DECISION I NEED TO MAKE

_____

_____

KNOW YOUR NO

As we walk into this exercise, I am going to ask you to imagine a situation at work and notice how your body responds. While I'm using guided imagery around work, my sense is that it will evoke the same bodily responses as if you were imagining a personal decision, but ultimately, you'll want to begin noticing the unique responses that your body has in certain situations.

Imagine the following. You are stuck in a job . . .

Working for your least favorite boss.

Working on a team composed of your five least favorite colleagues—the ones who drain you the most.

Working on the most boring, stress-inducing project you can imagine—a total energy sucker.

Working out of alignment with your values.

Working inside the most dull, chaotic workspace you've ever seen.

. . . and there's no way out of this scenario.

Holding this scenario in your mind now, where do you feel this in your body? Be specific about what you notice from head to toe.

Places in your body you notice: _____

_____

Sensations you notice: _____

_____

Colors you see or feel: _____

_____

Describe this feeling in a way you'll remember for future situations. Can you give it a name?

While every person feels their "no" in a different place, most of my clients report feeling tightness, constriction, or clenching in a certain part of their body—whether it's their jaw, neck, shoulders, stomach, or even in their extremities. Sometimes it feels extremely heavy or even like a prickling or burning sensation. There's no wrong way to feel to your no—what's important is that you know how your body talks to you.

I call my no a "steak on a grill" sensation—my stomach gets fiery and tingly just below my rib cage. Looking back, I can trace this feeling back to before I walked down the aisle with my first husband, to when I was trying to ignore red flags in my second relationship, and even in small life and career decisions I made that never worked out as I made up in my head. Recognizing this feeling ultimately helped me make my decision to leave corporate America. I was working for an author and leadership consulting firm at the time. I loved my job, my team, and my boss. They were a dream team, and on paper, everything looked A+ with salary and benefits to match. But there was a problem; every time my colleague would book my calendar for a travel engagement, my stomach would burn. Paying more attention to my body now at this point, I recognized that it wasn't the job itself or the work that was off—it was leaving my family for all the travel that pained me. I was newly married to my awesome husband, and my daughter was in middle school. I hated missing her activities and being away from home.

This burning feeling was surely inconvenient, but I couldn't ignore it. The data it was giving me was clear—get off the road. I worried and ruminated about telling my boss about my feelings. I didn't want to disappoint her, but I knew I couldn't live with disappointing myself either.

After a couple of months, I worked up the courage to tell her in our one-to-one meeting that I loved my work, but that I also couldn't make the amount of travel work any longer. I wanted to focus more on leadership coaching, an emerging part of my role that I loved and surged my energy. She was understandably disappointed but was incredibly supportive. After several conversations, she agreed to help me in any manner to either start my own coaching practice or find a corporate role with little to no travel. This conversation was difficult, but the relief of telling the truth gave me so much peace even though that choice looked much riskier on paper for me. And because I was honest with her and agreed to do my part in ensuring a smooth transition, she supported me in making a successful leap to entrepreneurship.

Look back over the course of your life: Have you felt this specific no feeling and chosen to ignore it, and gone instead with your logic, external advice, or data? How did this ultimately turn out for you?

My clients and I agree that when we've felt this feeling and ignored it, choosing instead to try to force something or do what we thought we "should" do, it never turned out well. When I was gut-wrenched about calling off my wedding, all the ignoring my stomach telling me "hell no" was leading to clenching and tension, causing my intestinal issues.

Shake this off. Let's find your yes.

EXPERIENCE YOUR YES

As we practice this exercise again, I will ask you to imagine a situation at work and notice how your body responds. While this continues to use guided imagery around work situations, my sense is that it will evoke the same bodily responses as if you were imagining a personal decision, but ultimately you'll want to begin noticing the unique responses your body has in certain situations.

Imagine the following. You are waking up in the morning, looking forward to a day of . . .

Working for your favorite leader, or the best leader you know or can imagine. You feel rewarded, seen, and heard.

Working in a team comprised of your five favorite, most supportive and uplifting colleagues.

Working on a project that makes your energy surge, using all your talents, something that excites you fully. You feel capable, fulfilled, and engaged.

Working inside an energetic yet relaxing work environment, one that feels safe and peaceful and aligned with your values.

. . . and you look forward to this every day.

Holding this scenario in your mind now, where do you feel this in your body? Be specific about what you notice from head to toe.

Places in your body you notice: _____

_____

Sensations you notice: _____

_____

Colors you see or feel: _____

_____

Describe this feeling in a way you'll remember for future situations. Can you give it a name?

While each person feels their "yes" in a different place, my clients and I report it feeling like openness, lightness, and an ease or relaxing in a certain part of their body—whether it's their jaw (smile), neck, shoulders, stomach, or even in their extremities. Sometimes it feels extremely airy or even the "good tingles" sensation. There's no wrong way to feel to your yes—what's important is you know how your body talks to you.

My yes feels like butterflies flying out from my chest—I call it my "fluttering" sensation. Earlier, I shared that my no was telling me to stop traveling, so I listened to my body to help me determine what my right next choice should be. Given that my boss and I decided that my time working for her would come to an end, I was faced with two choices: seek out another corporate role or take the leap and start my own business. Luckily, I had three months to explore and decide. In that period, I applied for two corporate roles and went to interviews. While one of the jobs sounded like a good fit for my values and talents, I couldn't shake the feeling of dread and tightness in my stomach when I walked into the office. When I imagined my days doing the work and driving to the office, I felt my stomach burn. Hell no.

Contrast that with starting my own coaching practice; there were many unknowns. While I would be able to retain one coaching contract through a joint agreement with my old boss, my income would be 30 percent of what I was earning in corporate America. There was no guarantee I would make a single extra dollar on top of my existing contract. My business could totally flop, and then I'd have to come crawling back into corporate life. (I had *lots* of *but firsts* running through my mind!) I also would have to set up my business, start a website, figure out how to find clients, and so many other uncertainties. The crazy thing was, amid all that uncertainty, I had the "heck yes" butterflies. I couldn't stop imagining myself starting a business doing something I loved—coaching and training. I felt pulled like a magnet to build my website and learn all I could about successfully starting a business. While it may not have made sense on paper financially or on a résumé, my gut was a yes. A heck yes. I couldn't *not* do it. Trusting myself has always paid off in my business decisions—everything from which business partners to hire to the programs I should offer to the clients I choose to work with.

Reflect again over the course of your life. Have you felt this specific yes feeling and chosen to follow it, even though it went against conventional wisdom or what was "expected" of you? How did it turn out for you?

Many people I've worked with, myself included, say following this feeling by moving forward has never let them down. They often say it preceded making the right decisions about their career, about people, or even about their plans. Starting my own business left me terrified in my mind, but my body was full of the good fizzy feelings—I couldn't help but move forward. I was scared and excited—scare-cited. I'm glad that chose entrepreneurship; while I've had challenges along the way, it's worked out better than I could have imagined.

Let's revisit the decision you wanted help with earlier.

DECISION I NEED TO MAKE

_____

_____

Imagine saying yes to this scenario, and everything that comes with that yes. Imagine yourself going through the motions of saying yes and then living out the results of this decision.

Places in your body you notice: _____

_____

Sensations you notice: _____

_____

Colors you see or feel: _____

_____

On scale of hell no to heck yes, mark a rating for this decision:

|——————————————————————————————————|
Hell no   Maybe   Heck yes

Imagine saying no to this scenario and everything that comes with that no. Imagine yourself going through the motions of saying no and then living out the results of this decision.

Places in your body you notice: _____

_____

Sensations you notice: _____

_____

Colors you see or feel: _____

_____

On scale of hell no to heck yes, mark a rating for this decision:

|———|

    Hell no   Maybe   Heck yes

No matter what, you should notice a difference in body sensations between the two feelings. At their basic difference, one decision should feel more constricting, and one should feel more open. One choice feels of dread; the other feels of peace. If you're anything like me, having first experienced an activity similar to this one that I learned from Martha Beck, you might be suddenly woken up to a whole new form of intelligence in your body. For me, I'd been disconnected from my body for so long, favoring instead my logical decision-making, that when I finally woke it back up, I felt flooded. I was suddenly overwhelmed feeling *everything in my body.* If this happens, have some compassion for yourself, and be patient with everything that your body is telling you. Slow down, practice naming your emotions, and ask your sensations what they want you to know.

Trusting your intuition is like a muscle: the more you practice it in low-stakes circumstances, the more you begin to notice subtle nuances that give you confidence for trusting your gut in higher-stakes moments. If you're having trouble discerning the difference or trusting this new source of information, practice tuning in to your body for small decisions—such as which route to take to work, what to choose from the menu, or what clothes to wear in a day. Notice what happens when you follow your gut versus what happens when your mind talks you out of it. The best way to practice using your intuition is to test the consequences of doing so, or not doing so, and seeing how it works for you.

CONNECT YOUR HEAD, HEART, AND GUT TO DECIDE WITH CLARITY

I believe the future of work will demand leadership programs that expand their focus and teach leaders more emotional and intuitive awareness. It will require leaders that lead with neck up and neck down intelligence. Researchers Grant Soosalu, Suzanne Henwood, and Arun Deo published a study in 2019 describing the decision-making experience and how humans use not just their head but all three brains to reach conclusions. We have the one we know and use in our head (one hundred billion neurons), another in our heart (forty thousand neurons), and another in our gut (one hundred million neurons). It bears repeating: the heart and gut create what people often consider to be their intuition.

The leaders of the future will need to trust their head *and* their heart and gut so they can lead and make decisions with more creativity, compassion, and confidence. If trusting your gut gives you a competitive advantage at work, then women have a leg up, says Dr. Daniel Amen, founder of the Amen Clinics. He says, "The female brain is wired for leadership." Women may exhibit more intuition, empathy, collaboration, self-control, and appropriate concern because of increased blood flow in the brain.

A woman's brain has evolved with a strong ability to organize environmental information and read nonverbal cues in others. For a research study, ninety thousand people were shown different photographs of people's eyes. They were then asked to say what they thought that person's mood was. The results: women consistently outperformed men. So not only are women highly educated and intellectually capable of leadership, they are better emotionally and intuitively wired for it.

You've learned everything you need so far in this book to use all three of your brains to fully trust your body and decide with clarity. You know how to use your head brain by gathering the facts and evidence and eliminating expensive thoughts. You've claimed your values, which is essential to listening to your heart brain. And now you've clued in to the sensations in your body, which is bringing clarity to the wisdom of your gut brain.

We can use all three brains in practice by using a **decision filter** that contains three aspects:

HEAD

What do I know for sure? What are the facts of the situation? What evidence do I have? What's my decision deadline? Starting with our head is the one that we use most frequently, and it's a good place to start. When making a decision, this is where the data, Excel spreadsheets, PowerPoint decks, or expert advice comes in handy. Our head makes a great chief operating officer or chief financial officer of our life, and it provides an opportunity for **creativity** by examining possibilities, evidence, connections, and future scenarios.

HEART

What are my values? Does this align with them? What emotions am I experiencing? What's their message? How do I want others to feel? Being grounded in our heart center of intelligence allows us to be **compassionate** and empathetic. Consider it to be your chief people and customer experience officer. Could you imagine experiencing the pandemic with a leader who was not in tune with their heart brain? Many successful leaders in difficult times know how to use empathy, attunement, and compassion to lead their teams. They also know the power of being connected to and compassionate with themselves.

GUT

What sensations do I feel in my body? Does this feel of peace or dread? Is this a heck yes or hell no? What is mine to do? Being grounded in this center of intelligence helps you listen to your body sensations and become in tune with your instincts. It's the place you may hear the still, small voice of your intuition when you quiet yourself and get intentional about listening to it. When aligned with your head and heart, it creates intentional action.

It creates **confidence** in action and decision. It makes for a good chief executive officer.

Putting this into practice, let's revisit the decision from above and run it through the decision filter.

DECISION I NEED TO MAKE

_____

_____

HEAD: What do I know for sure? What are the facts of the situation? What evidence do I have?

HEART: What are my values? Does this align with them? What emotions am I experiencing? What's their message? How do I want others to feel?

BODY: What sensations do I feel in my body? Am I getting a heck yes or hell no? Does this feel of peace or dread? What is mine to do?

My client Jen video-messaged me because she was feeling stuck in a moment of indecision. She's an executive leader for innovation at her firm and was feeling trapped in negotiating a stalemate between a desired vendor partnership she had been working to secure and the compliance demands of her organization. She wanted to win the partnership but was also concerned that this vendor's demands could tax the resources and not align with established policies of the organization. She didn't want to make either party upset but didn't want the negotiation to fail. She felt like she and her boss wanted different things. In moments like this, it's tempting to stay in neck-up awareness and focus solely on strategy, getting hooked by our ego and wanting to "win," and stuck in analysis paralysis of what-if scenarios. Knowing her leadership style, she knew she had a tendency to be overly assertive and not consider all sides before acting. So we slowed her down to check her head, heart, and gut.

I had Jen sit up in her chair with her feet on the floor and take a few deep breaths. We simply walked through her three brains for guidance. Taking a deep breath, I asked her to think about the evidence of the situation. What did she know for sure? What do the data and the numbers say? I encouraged her to drop any stories and remain focused on the facts of the business goals and the prospective client.

Taking another deep breath, I asked her to drop into her heart center. What were her values in this situation? What would acting in alignment with her values look like? What were the company's values? What values did they have in common? How did she want to feel during this negotiation? What three words described how she wanted the other parties to feel?

Taking another deep breath, I asked her to drop into her gut and give her intuition permission to give her wisdom here. I asked her to notice sensations in her body—did taking on this vendor feel like peace? Or of chaos? I asked her, "If your intuition or still, small voice had the answer, what would it say?" What's frustrating about this question is that our intuition often speaks to us in a few words. It doesn't reason with us—that's our ego. Intuition is a quiet nudge; ego is urgent and demanding. Intuition suggests; ego reasons and argues. Intuition feels of peace. Ego feels like fear.

While Jen told me that she stops to analyze things often, the act of checking in with her body and writing it down with a pen and paper gave her another layer of clarity. After her personal reflection, she knew the right answer and next steps as to how to communicate it. Jen reached out to her boss in an email and not only expressed the facts of the partnership in terms of data, revenue, and logic but also how it aligned with the organization's values. While she acknowledged to her boss that the prospect of the partnership brought a bit of nervousness and uncertainty, it felt more aligned with the excitement you feel that comes with growth and potential and not with dread that comes from taking on a client that doesn't align with their values. She presented two ways they could move forward with the partnership while also aligning to company policies.

Her boss agreed with her perspective, appreciated her thoughtful strategy, and gave the partnership a "go." Afterward, she felt confident, empowered, and excited about the decision and her ability to cut through the noise and make a profitable business recommendation based on trusting herself and not getting stuck in neck-up fears, others' opinions, or analysis paralysis. Trusting her gut allowed her to be thoughtful and strategic while also leading in her unique and assertive, but not pushy, way. This exercise helped her tap her creativity (head brain), her compassion (heart brain), and her confidence to take action (gut brain). Jen went on to tell me that she used this same practice to contribute to a higher level of confidence in a big presentation. She examined what was required of her in the presentation, how she wanted to be perceived, how to she wanted to feel, and what felt of peace to her in terms of her delivery style. She showed up as herself, wore bright colors, and spoke in a way that felt like her true voice. She received emails back from her board members complimenting her presentation and delivery style and expressing their excitement about the future of the organization. That's fully connected, intuitive, and authentic leadership power if I've ever seen it.

YOUR BODY IS TRUSTWORTHY

When we're looking to shift from chaos to clarity, here's a reminder that you can trust yourself. And if you're struggling to embrace that your body is trustworthy, let me ask you this: How old were you when you went on your first diet or realized you needed to change your looks? Were you between the ages of ten and fifteen years old? Many women tell me this, and I can relate. I was around age ten when I remember going on my first diet. I remember the clear messaging in TV commercials and in airbrushed images in my *YM* magazine of how I should look to be seen as an attractive or happy tween.

I was too young at the time to know that the diet industry was a *billion-dollar*-per-year industry that thrives upon showing women what they should look like and making them feel shame for how they actually look. In the early '90s, I learned I could drink two SlimFasts per day and eat a sensible dinner to lose weight, and how to ignore my hunger. I learned later on in my early thirties that excessive amounts of cardio and chewing gum were the best way to lose weight and keep your mouth busy so you don't eat. But I wasn't just learning how to lose weight and be a certain body type; I was unconsciously learning to numb myself—numb the pain by overexercising and also numb the intuitive cues to eat when I was hungry and stop when I was full. As an adult, overworking was also an excellent way I learned to numb out any feelings, emotions, or cues I had in my body.

Looking back now, it was clear that I second-guessed—or never even thought to trust—my gut because I was so busy criticizing, shaming, and numbing everything from the neck down. As women, we are subtly taught from a young age that our body can't be trusted. Too skinny. Too fat. Expose more skin. (Wait, you're showing too much.) We overwork and overwhelm our body, trying to make it fit others' standards because the beauty and diet industries are well versed at telling us our body "as is" is wrong. The unpaid workloads are high and hustle culture runs deep. While none of my diets worked over the long term, what they ultimately taught me is to ignore the natural rhythms, desires, and sensations in my body that cried for food, rest, compassion, and love.

After all, you can't numb all these desires and sensations in an effort to keep dieting or overworking without also numbing the wisdom from your intuition.

It's no wonder we don't slow down enough in our hustle culture and take time to listen to and trust our gut—as women, we've been taught to be experts at numbing it out by following the "rules" without questioning why. We are so busy overworking, overexercising, overdieting that we learn to shut down from the neck down, and then we try to make all our decisions from the neck up. This results in getting stuck in analysis paralysis and second-guessing.

All the while, our bodies are bursting with wisdom from our gut instincts, but we're too busy ignoring what our still, small voice already knows to be true.

Your body can be trusted. Your hunches. Your still, small voice. That subtle nudge in your gut that encourages you to check one more time, walk away, or make the phone call. She can be trusted. She is wiser than your best friend, the internet, the spreadsheet, and even your logical mind. **Your body is trustworthy.** She knows the difference between peace and dread, between a heck yes and hell no. Trusting yourself and your intuition is critical to having the confidence and clarity to make the right decision for *you*. Amid all the noise, it is your competitive advantage in leadership and life.

CLOSE THE CONFIDENCE GAP TOOL KIT

TRUST YOURSELF

NOTICE IT

Get intentional about taking time for quiet and scanning your body every day.

My heck yes sensation: _____

My hell no sensation: _____

OWN IT

1. Make a commitment to listen to your body before you make decisions: Ask, "How am I trusting myself in this decision?"
2. Practice checking in with your head, heart, and gut with small decisions so you have repetition and confidence going into the bigger decisions.

3. Keep a record: When have you trusted your gut and it's paid off (or vice versa)? What did your intuition know or nudge? What did you feel in your body?

ACT ON IT

Boost your peace, your potential, and your paycheck by having the courage to trust yourself and have courageous conversations.

1. Where do you need to trust yourself and make or communicate a potentially unpopular decision that you know is right?
2. Where do you need to be clear at work, or in life, about your yeses and noes?
3. Where might you need to reverse a decision you made, because you didn't listen to your gut before but now you are?

Visit CLOSINGTHECONFIDENCEGAP.COM/BOOKDOWNLOADS for a printable version of this tool or the entire workbook of tools in this book.

7

AMPLIFY YOUR VOICE AND MAKE AN IMPACT

Fight for the things you care about, but do it in a way that will lead others to join you.

RUTH BADER GINSBURG

n the early weeks and months of my new job at a healthcare technology firm, I sat around the table of leaders, wondering if they were questioning their hiring of me. After working for twelve years at the same organization, I'd made a career change from financial services to healthcare technology—finding an organization that was fully in alignment with my values and unique talents. There was no doubt in my mind that I'd found the right fit, even though I had no idea what they were talking about with their healthcare acronyms, technology algorithms, and consulting expertise. Some days I drove home thinking they could have been blending a script from *The Office* and *Grey's Anatomy,* and I would never know I was being punked.

Changing careers brought up unexpected difficulties, and the transition was harder than I expected. It was also confusing because I wanted the change, and I loved my colleagues and my new role overseeing human resources. I also was a beginner again, and that felt unexpectedly disorienting. In my old job, I'd worked in nearly every department of the regional bank over the course of twelve years and made solid connections. If I didn't know an answer, I always knew who to call. Whether I recognized it or not, it felt good to be known and in the know. Part of what helped me find my voice toward the latter end of my career at the bank came from owning an identity that I had created as an expert. Now I couldn't rely on any of that. I was a beginner again, both in relationships and in terminology. I didn't know my way around or who to call. It didn't feel good at all to be a beginner again—and I realized my ego was very wrapped up in my former identity as an expert and a knower. I just felt stupid.

Just as I started to figure out the networks, terminology, and acronym soup—feeling more comfortable to speak up in meetings, ask the right questions, and make contributions—our technology company was acquired by a publicly traded healthcare technology and staffing firm. The good news was that my CEO chose me to lead the integration, so while my human resources role was eliminated (surprise!), I would still have a role leading the integration and change management efforts. The bad news was that I found myself, yet again, sitting in conference rooms in another state with new executives, hearing inside conversations, topics, and acronyms I knew nothing about. I started to mentally form a list of *but firsts,* similar to the ones I shared in the imposter monster chapter, as I was feeling overwhelming doubt about speaking up. This made me even more critical of myself sitting in merger integration meetings with new senior executives, feeling completely useless with nothing to say.

I remember leaving the first day of integration meetings at the headquarters in San Diego, frustrated with myself (again) that I had so little to say or contribute. I worried that they would wonder: *Who brought her here? Why is she taking up a seat?* Sitting in my hotel room, I thought of all the things I wished I would have said during discussions or questions that I should have asked. I blamed myself again for being an introvert and wished I had the gift of easily verbalizing words and ability to quickly construct my thoughts and ideas.

I knew I was an introvert after some self-assessment work and reading the book *Quiet* by Susan Cain. This is surprising to people since the majority of my career was spent as a trainer and speaker, but what people don't consider is that I am not afraid of speaking in front of people, especially because my topics are thoughtfully researched, planned, and prepared. My strengths related to introversion include listening to conversations, reflecting, and asking good questions. I can better express myself in writing and am good at explaining ideas and concepts after I've had time alone to reflect and construct my story. Extroverts recharge by spending time with people, while introverts recharge by spending time alone. I don't process verbally like many extroverts do, and that's how organizations are built—they revolve around meetings, open-air workspaces when you're in the office, or talk-it-out brainstorming sessions meant to elicit ideas. But my brain doesn't work that way, and I know many other introverts who feel the same.

I think of all the good things to say *three hours after the meeting* when I've had some time to reflect and recharge. So there I was, making a list of all the ideas that came to me, and all the questions

I'd thought of asking but stayed quiet because I didn't want to look stupid. I realized I had two more days left of this three-day strategy session to make the impact I needed to make. I also had to own that this was *who I was*. I was not going to change into my more empathetic yet assertive boss or my endearing yet gregarious senior integration executive—ever. I always thought that maybe I needed to be more extroverted to be successful, but the truth was, I just needed to be my most authentic self to be successful. Whenever I tried to show up more extroverted, I just felt pressured, leading to more awkward and disjointed comments, not more effective dialogue. If I kept focusing on criticizing myself for not being extroverted, then I would be too insecure and distracted from showing up as *me*.

Well, who is *me*? I learned to ask myself an **authenticity** question that forever changed *how* I participate in meetings: *What do I know for sure about me?*

That evening in my hotel room, I wrote down all the reasons I could think of as to why my CEO wanted me at the strategy meetings and leading the integration project:

- I am good at leading change.
- I am good at building a new program and rolling it out to people.
- I am an expert at training and development.
- I am here to represent our people and future human resources interests.
- Because she believes in me and my talents.

After reflecting on this, I realized if I wanted to make an impact, I needed to own the reasons above, my unique talents, and claim my gifts of introversion—being a good listener and asking great questions. I realized I might not have all the answers in the discussion; there may even be times when they talk about things that are over my head. But I could add the unique perspectives I bring to the team—I could rely on my value of learning and ask questions in meetings to spark discussion or bring clarity to the changes that I would need to implement, identify the impacts on our people, or discern the type of training these initiatives would require.

I found some freedom in the revelation that I wasn't just there for me—I was there as an *advocate* for my entire group back in Nebraska. It suddenly felt easier to get out of my own head and ask and advocate on behalf of them in the meetings. In future meetings, owning my talents, asking good questions, and preparing for meetings through the lens of the unique perspective that only I could offer helped me to overcome feeling like an imposter and to find my voice. It was only the beginning.

YOUR VOICE MATTERS

"You're on mute."

If that wasn't the catchphrase while the corporate world fumbled with virtual meeting technology while switching from an in-person office to work from home during the pandemic, I don't know what was. Now that folks have figured out online meeting technology and are even moving back to in-person meetings, *are you on mute?* is actually a helpful self-coaching question. What do I mean by this?

- How many times do you have an idea or suggestion but stay silent because you're nervous about how people will react?
- Do you need to set a boundary or expectation but stay silent because you don't want the conflict?
- Do you want to start leading differently and use your voice as a leader but stay silent because you don't want to be perceived as too direct, bossy, or emotional?
- Are you overwhelmed by demands at work but stay silent because you don't want to be seen as a complainer?
- Do you want to contribute more but feel you must self-censor a bit because you are the only woman or person of color on the team?

Friend, if you're nodding your head to some of these, you're on mute. It's time to think about how remaining silent is costing you in your peace, potential, and your paycheck.

If you have an idea that you want to share but can't seem to find the confidence or the right words to say it, you are not alone. In a recent survey of eleven hundred US working adults, Catalyst, a nonprofit that works to accelerate women into leadership, found that 45 percent of women business leaders say it's difficult for women to speak up in virtual meetings, and one in five women say they've felt ignored or overlooked by colleagues during video calls.

Also, a joint study between University College London, Singapore University, the Indian Institutes of Management, and the University of Maryland looked at how often both women and men speak up in the workplace and found that women do in fact remain silent more frequently than men. They also found a solution: their study showed that women were more positively affected and gained more confidence when they saw women leaders speaking up, especially their direct supervisor. The reasons given behind this solution were that women relate to other women and desire to emulate their style in speaking up. Also, women reported that they could learn more on how to speak up from a female manager than from a male manager because the style of the female manager made them more comfortable.

Ultimately, the study recommended two important changes required in the workplace today. First, organizations need to hire and promote more women to boost confidence and encourage more women to speak up and be heard. Second, organizations need to actively encourage employees to contribute, and listen when they do.

Before we go any further with the *how* of amplifying your voice at work, it's important to address another reason *why* women hesitate to speak up at work. Psychological safety. Amy Edmonson, author and professor at Harvard Business School, describes psychological safety as a shared belief held by team members that the team is a safe environment for interpersonal risk taking. When employees feel safe, they trust that they can admit mistakes, seek feedback, or even fail without dire consequences. Teams with psychological safety are more innovative, growth-oriented, collaborative, trustworthy, and inclusive. A two-year study at Google found that feeling secure enough to contribute was by far the most common feature of high-performing teams.

Edmonson also says that women are less likely than men to speak up without solid data or the conviction that they're definitely right about what they're going to say. In alignment with the University of Maryland study previously discussed, Modupe

Akinola, associate professor of management at Columbia, tells us that when you are "the only one"—whether it be the only woman in the room or the only minority—you will feel greater pressure to self-censor because the environment makes you feel less safe.

If you are a leader of people, you have a responsibility to ensure everyone's voices are heard. Notice when women or people of color are talked over when trying to share their ideas, and ask them to take the floor to share their full idea. One of my clients, Dana, experienced the power of this recently. As the only female leader in a room of male senior executives and company vendors, she could not get a word in edgewise, and her male colleague continued to dominate the meeting. The vendor, noticing that she was continually talked over, stepped in and said, "Dana, it sounds like you have an idea that I'd love to hear." Make sure everyone gets a chance to speak. Most importantly, ensure you are hiring diverse team members.

If you are working in an environment that doesn't feel psychologically safe, you always have agency on making the right choice for you. You may have options to approach trusted colleagues or human resources to discuss the issue. If your attempts have not been heard and addressed, it may be time to consider making a change. Your voice matters, your ideas deserve to be heard, and you are worthy of contributing your full potential, without feeling like you must self-censor every day (how exhausting).

If your voice deserves to be heard, then how do you handle interruptions? My friend Brooke once worked on a team of six women, all in their sixties, who would not leave a single beat of silence in hours-long meetings. She had been trained never to interrupt, and it made it very difficult for her to speak up. So what do you do if you find yourself sitting in a room of talkers and don't want to be rude about interrupting? Brooke recommends the same advice I give to my clients: if it's a frequent occurrence, address it individually with the leader and ask for your time on the floor. In healthy work cultures, it's important to remember that extroverts don't often consider interruptions rude—they see you as joining the conversation. By contrast, there are real moments when women find themselves interrupted or spoken over. You can reclaim your power by simply saying, "I'd like to finish my thought."

CHOOSE CONNECTION OVER PERFECTION

Every night my husband and I require our daughter to come upstairs and hang out with us for a bit—something we call mandatory family fun time. She was a freshman in high school, so it was getting easier for her to stay busy with her friends, technology, and homework and head straight to her room after dinner. One evening she stomped up the stairs and plopped into the chair. I asked her my two standard questions: "How was your day? What homework do you have?"

She sighed. "Ugh. *Fine. Mom*—tomorrow I have to stand up and give a five-minute talk in English class, and I'm so stressed out. I get nervous when I'm up there because everyone is staring at me. Then my neck and face get red, so I get even more nervous, and then I start to read from my note card. And if I read from my note card, my teacher will dock my grade down to a B. *Ugh*, I hate this, and I don't want to do it! I hope she forgets to call on me tomorrow."

My husband shot me a look that basically said, *you got this one, dear.* "Oh, honey!" I replied to her. "I know how nerve-wracking it feels to get up in front of people. I still get nervous even after all my years of training and speaking. What makes you most scared about tomorrow?"

After giving it some thought, she said, "I just hate how they all sit there and stare at me. They're judging me, and it makes me nervous."

"I understand," I replied. "But let me ask you this: When your classmates are up there giving their speeches, what are *you* doing and thinking about?"

She paused. A big smile grew on her face, and she giggled. "I'm not really thinking of them, Mom. I'm only sitting there thinking of myself, rehearsing my own speech in my head, or daydreaming about lunch."

She instantly relaxed, and so did I. I've been a corporate trainer and now a public speaker for a total of fifteen years of my life. I still get nervous, and that part is normal. But the freeing wisdom in my daughter's revelation that evening is also true—nobody is thinking of us as much as we think they are. They are only thinking of themselves. We are only thinking of ourselves and our own nerves, doubt, and imposter feelings.

My daughter helped me highlight something so important—we are all just busy thinking of our own issues and missing opportunities for connection. In my experience, I get tripped up preparing my presentations and conversations with worries such as, *What should I say? How will that sound? What's the right approach? What should I say first, next, and last? What data do they want? What if they think all this is stupid?*

How often do we stop and remember that these are real people we are talking to? I learned to ask myself **alignment** questions to create connection: *What approach aligns to my values? How do I want them to* feel?

Stopping and remembering that there are two people in this exchange and becoming intentional about the energy you want to create helps shift your focus from ruminating on your worries to cultivating a connection.

One of my clients, Cara, came to our coaching call nervous about how she was going to approach a difficult conversation she needed to have with one of her employees. While she enjoyed having this person on her team, their performance was inconsistent at best. Cara needed to have a difficult performance conversation, including feedback on specific behaviors along with a written action plan. Cara was wrecked and feeling anxious about what to say and how to say it. I asked Cara to reflect on her core values that we'd defined earlier in our relationship, which were fun, mastery, flexibility, honesty, and love. "How can you have this conversation honestly and lovingly?"

A light turned on; she had some ideas that she quickly wrote down.

Then I asked, "How do you want this employee to *feel* when you are having this conversation?"

Her whole body relaxed. "I want them to feel seen, supported, and clear on actions to take."

Aligning her values with how she wanted her employee to feel helped her redirect her energy away from her nerves and into making a connection in her conversation so she could get the outcome that served both of them well.

This works for big presentations too. My then fourteen-year-old taught me a valuable lesson that changed how I prepare for every presentation. As I build my slides for a webinar or a company workshop, I still think about the first **authenticity** question I posed earlier in this chapter: *What do I know for sure about me?* I let that guide the topics that I cover or expertise I can offer. Then I ask the **alignment** question: *How do I present this in alignment with my values? How do I want my audience to feel?* The alignment question shifts my focus from doubt and worrying about what people think to getting curious about creating an experience that makes them feel seen, confident, and inspired.

WHAT IS MINE TO SAY?

There are issues in our lives and in our work that are so vulnerable, so tender that it can be easier just to sweep them under the rug and remain silent. At work, you may be called to voice your opinion on a controversial decision. In the days I oversaw human resources, I'd often have to explain to our staff why we made a difficult decision that impacted their careers or benefits. Sometimes you'll need to give tough feedback or share hard news in the most compassionate, respectful way possible. Some days, you may have so much to say about an issue that you may need to know when to stay quiet. I have yet to experience an opportunity to speak up with an idea, share my experiences, or hold a tough conversation that didn't require vulnerability.

I had some heart-wrenching practice with figuring out what to say about an important topic for many women. When my husband and I married in 2018, we never thought we'd spend the first few years of our marriage struggling with infertility. Before I met Jason, I had my beautiful daughter, Hailey, without any issues. After Hailey was born, I miscarried at fifteen weeks, at eight weeks, and then had an ectopic pregnancy. My first marriage ended in 2011. Despite my past struggles, I was confident our luck would be different. It wasn't. We were shocked that after a year of trying, I wasn't pregnant, so we had our OB/GYN run tests— everything was normal (which, by the way, is super frustrating to hear—you want to be able to fix something!). We were lucky enough to have infertility insurance through Jason's employer, so we met with a reproductive endocrinologist about our options.

We decided to move forward with IVF—I had *zero* clue what I was in for! As someone who likes to plan, there is nothing you can plan with IVF. The shots. The mixing medicines. The unpredictable appointments. And the hormones, OMG. I alternated between feeling like I was on adrenaline or so exhausted that I couldn't function past 7:00 p.m. Unfortunately, the three rounds of IVF did not go as planned. The first round did not produce a viable embryo. The second round produced two viable embryos: one boy and one girl. We transferred the first embryo in May 2020 after being delayed three months by the pandemic while every clinic was in lockdown, which was equally as difficult. I was thrilled to find out I was pregnant in June, only to miscarry two weeks later. We still had hope the second embryo would finally be our baby. We transferred that embryo in September 2020 and were devastated to learn that it didn't "stick." We were beyond crushed and utterly deflated. In both cases, I sobbed and felt in a daze for weeks. Thank God for my therapist, who helped me through my grief. While we made the difficult decision not to continue with IVF, we were shocked to learn that I got pregnant on my own in March 2021, only to miscarry, again, one week later.

We could try IVF again but decided we'd done more than we ever planned to do to have a family and were coming to terms that kids aren't in the plan for us. My husband and I had to trust ourselves, not the advice of others, when our guts told us a *heck no* when we thought about trying another round of IVF. This was hard when my small-town Catholic-school upbringing taught me that society not only expects but somewhat defines a successful marriage by the ability to have kids. I had to learn that a positive pregnancy test is *not* a success stick when it comes to marriage and family. We are lucky to have found each other, and Jason is a wonderful stepdad to Hailey.

Why is it mine to share such a personal story? First, fertility is not a niche issue. One in eight women of reproductive age experiences problems when trying to conceive a child. This makes infertility about as common as breast cancer and more common than type 2 diabetes. And yet discussing such matters, especially in the workplace, is taboo. My friends have shared stories of sneaking out to meet their partners in the company parking lot to administer hormone shots. They've had to fake illnesses to get the time off to make fertility monitoring appointments. Many women resort to suffering in silence and taking a hit to their confidence for fear of being labeled, because of gender bias, as "unreliable" or "too emotional." Without IVF, conceiving a baby for heterosexual couples is an intimate and personal experience. You can hide the process until you are several weeks along and make an announcement on your terms.

For women, the IVF journey is so much more taxing than hiding emotions and sneaking off to appointments. When workplaces have no clear policies on the kind of support they offer to those undergoing fertility treatments, this creates a culture of silence and stigma. A culture of openness, understanding, and support needs to be nurtured. Then, perhaps, women—and their partners—wouldn't feel as isolated during their IVF journeys. I felt frustrated, and I know I'm not alone.

Since I had left corporate America and was running a coaching practice whose mission was to help women advance to the rooms where decisions are made, I felt a burning desire to be a voice for women on this issue. I could make some purpose out of my pain. National Infertility Awareness Week comes every year in April, which gave me a window of opportunity to share my story so other women knew they weren't alone and to advocate to employers on policies that would help their women leaders stop hiding and start thriving.

Sharing such a personal issue is hard, and it would just be easier to remain silent, but I felt power in owning my **authentic** story and point of view. I was also representing others who were struggling with the same disease. The approach of sharing it in writing felt in **alignment** with my values. I wanted women struggling with infertility to *feel* seen, heard, and embraced.

This opportunity to share my story brought me to my third and final **action** question that comprises my framework to amplify your voice: *Based on my values, what is mine to say (or not say)?*

As a reminder, my values are love, respect, family, creativity, and learning. I asked myself: How can I share my story in a *loving* way? How can I write it that feels *respectful* of my husband's feelings too? How can I advocate for *families*—no matter how they are composed? Finally, it was important to me to talk to organizations to support women—what can they *learn* to help them empower women to show up fully at work? (This aligned with my mission.) With these questions in mind, I published my story to *Working Mother* magazine and HuffPost. Shondaland acquired the story rights as well. I recorded and published a podcast and two video interviews with other women leaders experiencing infertility to bring awareness and conversations to the workplace.

It never ceases to amaze me the amount of hurtful, judging, and uniformed comments that people will leave on a tender post when it's shared to social media. This is why speaking your voice in alignment with your values is so critical. We can't control what other people will think, do, or say. Author of *The Four Agreements*, Don Miguel Ruiz, reminds us, "Nothing others do is because of you. What others say is a projection of their own reality." We don't know what dramas other people are working through and what causes them to respond to our actions the way they do. But speaking up in alignment with our values is something we can control. It's helped me use my voice and share my story with integrity. Using my values to guide my words gave me the courage to share something so personal without second-guessing myself or focusing on negative reactions.

This action question also helps you determine when to speak up or stay silent at work. My extroverted clients love this question, because they often don't struggle with speaking up during open brainstorming. They struggle with speaking up *on everything*. Then, because they've spoken up on everything, they tend to take on too much, feel overwhelmed, and regret being such a talker. At least this is what my client Kristen tells me. Kristen is a powerful and energetic community leader. Not only is she the executive director of her organization, but she is also involved in several community nonprofit organizations. Kristen has thoughts and new ideas about everything, and in many of our calls, we spent time talking about how to respond to an abundance of project requests or the latest executive board meeting. Kristen would often joke with me that she'd offer her opinion on just about everything, but sometimes that caused unwanted drama in her life. It became stressful, especially because she found people wanting more of her time to gossip.

Kristen started using this action question before every meeting: *Based on my values, what is mine to say? What is mine NOT to say?* This level of clarity helped her get clear on where her contributions would have the best return on investment, based on her values and goals. It also helped her remain quiet on issues that weren't in her area of expertise or had no bearing on her working initiatives. It gave others more opportunity to contribute and take on projects. Ultimately, it helped Kristen be a more effective and focused leader in her time, energy, and people circle. She admits, "I think people used to tune me out because I was speaking up on everything. Now I reserve my energy and contributions for the *right things*, and I've noticed that people stop and engage in more thoughtful dialogue. I've learned that some things are just not mine to say and someone else can do it better. So I let them."

THE ADVOCACY MODEL

When you're facing high-stakes situations and don't know what to say or how to say it, or you are ready to speak up and share your thoughts and ideas, the advocacy model can help you feel and speak more confidently on what is yours to say. I've personally used this model to design speaking programs and to guide how I will speak up on social media or in writing on women's leadership issues. I used this very model to write the book you're reading.

My clients have used this model to guide feedback and coaching conversations, high-stakes presentations, and even job interviews.

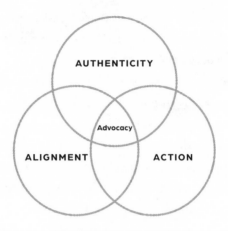

AUTHENTICITY QUESTIONS

- What do I know for sure about me?
- What are my unique talents and skills?
- What or who am I also representing?

ALIGNMENT QUESTIONS
(LIST THREE ADJECTIVES FOR EACH)

- What do I value here?
- How do I want to be seen?
- How do I want others to feel?

ACTION QUESTIONS

- How am I being clear about what I want or need?
- What is mine to say (or not say)?
- What is mine to do?

THE FOUR Cs OF SPEAKING UP

A final note about the *action* part of speaking up. One of the skills women tell me they want to refine as they advance at work is their presentation skills. This is especially important as you increase your exposure in your organization or community. With a higher-level audience, the stakes rise and the time shortens to show up confidently, deliver a clear message, make the asks you need, or deliver a high-impact message. This heightened level of exposure to new leaders and audiences can bring more doubt, nerves, and even imposter feelings, and that's not surprising. Studies show that 75 percent of the population fears public speaking in some form, where it be a slight nervousness at the very thought of public speaking to full-on panic and fear.

Just one difficult presentation can deal a blow to your confidence, so how do you show up, speak up, and create the impact you want to make? Over my fifteen years of speaking and training experience, I've learned there are four Cs for presenting well:

Be Clear: What outcome do you want from this meeting? Design your message for this, and say it at the beginning. As mentioned already, people are horrible guessers, so be clear about what you want and why you're presenting. Success loves clarity here.

Be Concise: If you have one hour, a good rule of thumb is to keep your presentation to no more than three topics. For every fifteen minutes, try to keep it to one topic. People have short attention spans, and too many topics may send your audience down the wrong trail, or you risk losing their attention altogether.

Be Connected: Instead of obsessing over your nerves, remember to focus instead on how you want your audience to feel. What's the "so what" factor for them in your message? What's in it for them? Tailor your presentation accordingly.

Be Confident: Own your talents and point of view. You are there for a reason. Practice and know the "bottom-line themes" of your presentation. It's okay and normal for you to feel nerves while also delivering with confidence (I do all the time!). The actions of confidence come first, the feelings come second. This is a great time to remember the advice from the Taming Your Imposter Monster chapter: you can deliver an effective presentation *while also* feeling nervous.

> When you speak up, you inspire others to do the same.

YOU DON'T NEED TO "FIND" YOUR VOICE

In celebration of our first wedding anniversary, my husband and I took a quick trip to the Florida Keys. With an afternoon to fill, we stopped at the Turtle Hospital on Marathon Key. It was a Tripadvisor recommendation, and we had three extra hours, so despite our concerns that we may not enjoy it, we signed up for the tour anyhow. If anything, we'd enjoy touching some giant sea turtles. Upon entering the main facility, we were brought to a room with a large video screen and chairs. "Oh great," I thought, "a boring science lesson."

But I was wrong. The tour guide proceeded to share fascinating statistics about sea turtles, how pollution contributes to their declining birth rate, and the bumps on their shells and skin. Then the tour guide dropped this gem: Sea turtles will only give birth on the beach where they were also born. They can find their way back to this beach despite having swum tens of thousands of miles away.

Okay, I was in full geek-out enjoyment mode and as curious as the third grader sitting next to me. I raised my hand: "How in the world do they find their way back?" (I mean, I can't find anything without GPS these days.)

The tour guide said the earth's coastline has a magnetic signature and that sea turtles have an internal compass of sorts that reads this magnetic data so they can find their way. "But there's a real problem," said the tour guide. "With all the oceanic pollution from noise and materials, the birth rate is going down because pollution interferes with their inner compass's ability to connect with the magnetic reading that would lead them home."

Mind. Blown. After the presentation, we went on to see the turtles in surgery and touch and feed those swimming in the pools. But I couldn't stop thinking about this story. I mean, if God, our Creator, the Universe, whoever, put this sort of inner compass ability in a turtle to find their way home, just imagine what's inside us. If you caught the news in 2020, there was a record number of sea turtles on beaches because the pandemic dramatically reduced oceanic pollution. More turtles were finding their way home due to less interference.

If you noticed that I didn't give you specific tips or recommendations on *how* you should amplify your voice to make an impact at work in this chapter, you're correct. There is no one right way to use your voice. Trying to sound more like your boss won't help you make an impact. Striving to conform to a set of adjectives (for example, direct, gregarious, funny, visionary) won't help you make the impact you were born to make; it will simply create interference. It keeps you distracted from showing up as your true self.

Like a sea turtle looking for home, you don't "find" your voice by looking at and trying to mimic everyone else or a certain standard. The voice you need to make an impact is already inside you, and it will be revealed when you remove what's standing in the way of it.

CLOSE THE CONFIDENCE GAP TOOL KIT

AMPLIFY YOUR VOICE AND MAKE AN IMPACT

Message or idea I want to share:

NOTICE IT

Notice where you have ideas but are placing yourself on mute or allowing your but firsts to get in the way.

Notice if any environments trigger your need to stay silent more than others, or by contrast, cause you to overshare.

OWN IT

Here are a few more questions to help you craft your message, based on the advocacy model.

Authenticity

- What are the facts of the situation? What value do I bring?
- What is critical for them to know?

Alignment

- What do I value in this situation or conversation? Who is hearing it, and what do they value?

Action

- What's mine to say, and how can I say it in alignment with my values?
- When will I communicate this?
- What action do I want them to take because of this conversation?

REFRAME IT

It's easy to get caught up and focus on our own nerves, doubts, and mistakes. How do you want others to feel when receiving your message?

ACT ON IT

Boost your peace, your potential, and your paycheck by being clear, concise, and confident in your message. Take yourself off mute and focus on connecting with your audience.

What is my plan and approach to communicate and make an impact using the advocacy model? Write it out.

Visit CLOSINGTHECONFIDENCEGAP.COM/BOOKDOWNLOADS for a printable version of this tool or the entire workbook of tools in this book.

8

KNOW YOUR WORTH

We all know that women, on average, are paid less for the same work than men. I absolutely believe, however, that directors should demand and review fully transparent compensation analysis and hold the CEO accountable for getting to pay parity. It's about time.

INDRA NOOYI

on't talk about your salary. I'm not sure where the origins of the *don't talk about your salary* rule started, but it fostered a long-standing issue inside the organization I worked for and in nearly every firm in America. This rule started long before I received my first paycheck; years earlier, I had learned it in my own home. I was a curious kid who also didn't mind asking my parents about adult topics, like budgeting, how much their house payment was, how and why my baby sister was born so many years after me, and how much money they made at work. I can still hear my mother's well-meaning words to me: "Honey, it's not polite to talk about money, and you definitely shouldn't ask people what they make."

Money fascinated me, but as a little girl my only career goal was to be a television meteorologist. I loved talking about weather and studying weather patterns and declared it my major in college. By rule, talking about the weather is considered to be the safest topic to discuss. Then my mother switched careers from speech pathology to investing—she was recruited by an investment firm to be a financial advisor. With a new mindset around talking money, she sat down one weekend with me while I was in college and showed me a little paper slider tool that demonstrated how much money you would have at retirement if you invested $50, $150, or $250 every month. The numbers had lots of zeros, so I was fascinated. Sure, I'd learned about the time value of money in business courses, but not like this.

Recognizing the importance of future money and now evaluating career-choice salary opportunities, I changed my major of meteorology (besides, I didn't like all the calculus and physics classes) to political science and business. I also reconsidered my college job. I was working at a retail store in the mall, but a coworker told me she also had a job at a national bank that paid well, closed up by 5:30 p.m., and paid full tuition reimbursement. I was intrigued, so I applied and got the job. I not only earned a small per-hour raise but also enjoyed free money for college tuition. I also worked very part-time at the same investment firm that hired my mom. I learned about the stock market, investing, retirement funds, savings vehicles, and the importance of managing debt—which I failed at miserably in my twenties and thirties, which contributed to my kitchen-table meltdown.

After college graduation, I spent the next twelve years of my life working in investments and banking. Yes, it was fun to learn about money at the fifty-thousand-foot level, but there was a topic that I discovered in my variety of human resources roles that I obsessively researched, observed, and coached candidates through—how to talk about salary and ask for money in raises and job offers.

In one of my first human resources roles, I was in charge of onboarding new employees on their first day. This meant that all their documents were signed properly, including their offer letters. I walked around the conference room and picked up the signed offer letters from the newly hired employees: $125,000. $250,000. $175,000. $75,000. It wasn't the salaries themselves that were a surprise to me. I knew that was the market rate for their job role at the time. What kept me awake at night was recognizing the pay disparity between employees newly hired into our organization and legacy employees in nearly the same role, with the same level of experience.

It was just the beginning of the pay disparity I'd see across the organization, especially in senior leadership roles. Another issue that I began to spot was that most of the senior-level roles were being filled by men. I didn't have language for it at the time, but the difference in pay between newly hired male leaders and their female counterparts was what I've now come to know as the gender pay gap. There was no standard mechanism in the organization to bring up salaries from long-standing employees to match the rates of the newly hired leaders.

There was another insider secret I learned from my time in human resources—the importance of negotiating your salary and how infrequently women held these conversations. Many of my HR years were spent recruiting and managing negotiations between the candidate and my employer. I also spent time talking employees through annual raises, coaching them through approaching their manager about a raise or promotion. In this role, I noticed a stark difference between male and female candidates—men mostly negotiated their pay offers and women did not. In addition, men tended to have higher starting salary requirements than women.

As a human resources professional, I was part of the problem. We had rules in our organization, as do many organizations, that didn't allow us to make large jumps in someone's salary. The maximum raise each year averaged around 3 percent, and if you changed roles or were promoted in the organization, they frowned upon increasing your salary beyond 15 percent. All these years later, when I am talking with my clients who are navigating a promotion or a raise, they cite these same rules as to why they are being paid below their peers or the market rate.

For me personally, recognizing the limits of the 3 percent annual raise cap made it rewarding for me to continually switch roles inside my organization. Every two years, when I started to get bored in my current role at the time, I had three choices: 1) stay bored and do nothing, 2) ask for more projects or find a way to spice things up, or 3) check out the job postings board for a higher-grade position that would provide not only a new challenge to ease my boredom, but also a change to make a bigger salary jump.

Because the cost of living and skyrocketing insurance costs were accelerating faster than the standard 3 percent increase (and if you were a high-performing employee who received 4 or 5 percent, it wasn't much better), it cost me money to stay in the same role. And still, many people who loved their jobs stayed in the same role year after year, only to earn marginal increases and to be passed up by outsiders who joined the organization.

What I know for sure after all my years working in human resources and with clients who are making career changes is this: money feels like one big secret at work, and not enough women like to talk about it. But talking about money isn't shameful; it's essential for women to close the pay gaps.

Money should be as easy to talk about as the weather.

CLOSE THE MONEY GAPS

Reality check. If you're a woman, and you've never asked for a raise or negotiated your salary upon hire, you are likely working the equivalent of three unpaid months out of every year while your male counterpart enjoys nearly 20 percent more in earnings. This problem is the gender pay gap. While the exact pay gap ranges differ based on the research study, the US Census Bureau identifies that white women only earn 80 to 82 percent of what men earn. Black women earn 63 percent of what a man earns, and Latinx women earn just 57 percent. Given today's pay gap reality, a twenty-year-old beginning full-time work today stands to lose $406,760 over a forty-year career compared to her male counterpart. If you dig into the averages, you'll see that women of color still lose more ground, with Black women losing over $900,000 and Latinx women losing over $1,000,000.

Does money really matter all that much when it comes to confidence? Experiencing the effects of the gender wage gap on a daily basis can be exhausting for women, and it can feel out of your control, especially when so much of our confidence comes from our work. The feelings of frustration often become internalized, which can lead women to feel depressed and anxious, says Maureen Sayres Van Niel, psychiatrist and president of the American Psychiatric Association Women's Caucus.

A 2016 study from Columbia University looked at the mental health consequences of gender wage gaps and found that when women make the same amount or more than their male counterparts (who are equally qualified for their jobs), their likelihood of experiencing depression and anxiety are about the same. But when women make less money, they're 2.4 times more likely to experience depression and 4 times more likely to have anxiety.

This creates a double bind for women. The Wharton research on the confidence gap indicates that women are less likely to self-promote, leading to lower salary offers. Then that lower-than-market salary impacts her confidence and well-being. But it's not just on women to close the gender pay and wealth gap; governments and corporations must examine their systems and policies to improve transparency and remove the barriers to pay equity.

Is it time for more girls' nights and money talk? Why not? About 52 percent of women say they talk about money with friends, compared to 61 percent of men, according to U.S. Bank. This is important because the more women get comfortable talking about money, both in their personal finances and with employers, the better chance there is to reduce the gender pay gap and investment gap. There are five conversations that every woman needs to be a part of to own her worth, ask for what she deserves, and close the gender money gaps: challenge the **systems**, notice your **self-talk**, negotiate your **salary**, evaluate your **savings**, and ask for **support**.

CONVERSATION 1:
CHALLENGE THE SYSTEMS

When you applied for your last job, were you required to disclose your salary history information? If you live in most states, this is likely the case. This is one of the first places that gender-based salary discrepancies begin. The logic is that because women and people of color have traditionally been paid less than white men, this trend would continue if employers were basing a starting salary on one's previous salary instead of offering the market rate. Nineteen states have passed a bill banning this ask, and hopefully the remaining thirty-one will follow. I've personally written to my state legislature supporting Nebraska's efforts in banning this requirement and encourage you to do the same.

What can you do if you're required to give your salary history? Provide it while also having a transparent conversation with the recruiter that you believe you have been underpaid and clearly state the desired salary you're looking for (more tools to come for you on that conversation!).

Pay and compensation systems exist in most organizations, but it's a big secret to those outside human resources. According to the Institute for Women's Policy Research, 75 percent of workers are discouraged or prohibited from discussing wages and salaries. However, according to the National Labor Relations Act and employees covered underneath it, it is not illegal to discuss wages. While money tends to be a private topic for most people, this transparency gap creates inequities. Research compiled by a leading compensation firm, World at Work, argues for pay transparency, and when organizations make wages visible to employees, businesses cannot hide structural inequalities that result from gender discrimination. They also found that pay transparency, which varies from organizations like Whole Foods posting actual salaries to those clearly posting approved compensation ranges for roles, results in increased team cohesion, diversity, and productivity.

Women can start these conversations at work by asking their organization about their compensation structure and philosophy. You can also ask the recruiter what the pay range is for the role you are applying for. I encourage my clients to ask organizations about their diversity metrics, including the pay gap, and how the organization works to address it. If you are a leader, the best place to begin is by evaluating and correcting any inequities in your own team and sharing your progress with your colleagues.

CONVERSATION 2:
NOTICE YOUR SELF-TALK

I had a client come to me completely frustrated. She had just discovered that she was making significantly less than a male peer on her team for doing nearly identical work. She did some additional salary market research and also determined in fact that she should be paid about $10,000 more annually to be in line with market ranges. She went on to tell me about some of the recent improvements she'd made in her department and the results her company had seen from it. She was deeply hurt that her salary didn't feel like a reflection of her worth.

Not knowing all the details and background, I asked her, "What happened when you asked for your raise?"

She put her head in her hands. "I haven't asked." When we got to the bottom of her reason for not asking, she admitted, "I feel like I shouldn't have to ask. They should just know, right?"

There are so many messages we've been taught as women about asking, and these tend to rear their ugly head when it comes time to ask for a raise or promotion. My own inner money talk track that holds me back is *Money is tight, so I shouldn't ask.* I often hear expensive thoughts, which widen the confidence gap, from other women:

- I should just be grateful for what I have.
- If I ask, I'll look pushy or demanding.
- It's impolite to ask or talk about money.
- It's selfish to put myself first here when others have more pressing needs.

What self-talk holds you back from talking about money? Unfortunately, our negative inner talk track or cultural upbringing gives us lots of reasons and stories for not asking. The real question is, Do those reasons lead us to the results we want? Not asking is an expensive habit, which costs us again in our peace, our potential, and especially in our paycheck.

You are worth asking for.

Here's the thing: you are worth asking for, just as you are. Do not confuse your net worth and your self-worth—your self-worth is nonnegotiable. This is exactly the confident mindset that my client took into her salary negotiation: *I am worth asking for.* She presented the market salary data for her role, demonstrated her recent success and business results, and made a successful ask for a salary adjustment.

The negative self-talk related to doubt and imposter feelings can hold you back from the higher-paid roles you are fully capable of doing but hesitating to apply for. Because women tend not to apply for jobs unless they feel they possess each of the listed qualifications, the result is that a man will more readily apply to roles that have a higher salary, because he'll have the confidence to do so despite not meeting all the job criteria.

According to several recruiters in my network, and in my own human resources experience, when women do apply for a higher-level job, they tend to possess the belief that since they aren't meeting 100 percent of the job criteria or experience, they'll rationalize a lower salary offer instead of a salary based on fair market pay or the value they bring to the company. My personal experience as a hiring manager and HR professional confirms much of what the data reveals—women ask for less, hesitate to apply, and negotiate less often than men. Women spend far too much time believing the lie they are unqualified, unworthy, or not ready. We can easily list ten reasons in our head why we shouldn't take on a new challenge that could result in a promotion, bonus, or additional income.

CONVERSATION 3: NEGOTIATE YOUR SALARY

In my early twenties, when I was moving to Nebraska from Missouri, I was applying for several jobs. I interviewed for, and was offered, a role at the bank I'd stick with for the next twelve years of my life. Did I take my own money advice that I'd started to learn from my mother and negotiate my salary? Nope. Sure didn't. I was happy to be offered a job and was even more thrilled that the salary offer was 30 percent more than my previous job. I didn't have the awareness at the time to know if it was in market range, but what I know today is that the first starting salary at that organization set the trajectory for my pay for the next twelve years. How often have you accepted the first salary offer, simply because it was an increase over your current pay? One of the core reasons a gap exists is because women do not take the initiative to negotiate their salary, putting them at an immediate salary disadvantage to their male peers.

According to a study by Linda Babcock and her colleagues, male graduates from Carnegie Mellon University had starting salaries 7.6 percent higher than women. While the initial salary *offer* was similar, 57 percent of the men negotiated their salary offer, as compared to only 7 percent of the women. Men initiate salary conversations *four* times more often than women, and when women do negotiate, they ask for 30 percent less than their male counterparts. Some women tell me that negotiating for more makes them feel pushy. You are not being greedy or pushy if done tactfully, in alignment with your values, and with an honest assessment of how you can help your company succeed.

CONVERSATION 4:
EVALUATE YOUR SAVINGS

My husband is a financial advisor (have I told you that I literally can't get away from money talk?), and he likes to joke around with his male clients that their wife—if they are married to a woman—is a better investor than they are. This makes them laugh a little nervously, as many stereotypes persist that men are better with money than women. So he likes to share with them some research published by Wells Fargo and Ellevest that shows that women tend to get better average returns, even though they tend to have two-thirds less money saved than men. This is known as the wealth gap. Don't believe the myth that men are just better with money; it's important for women to pay attention too. Also, women tend to outlive men by six to eight years, so they must make their retirement dollars stretch longer. What many financial advisors will tell you is that women often find themselves learning to manage money late into retirement—they are newly in control when their male partners pass away.

Thinking beyond today into your future, a study by *Money* magazine revealed that women's retirement savings balances are 50 percent less than men's—even though they even save at a higher percentage of income. Correspondingly, because a woman tends to make less, it means that if her company offers a matching 401(k) retirement program, her company-funded match is less than a man's. Simply stated, men get a higher amount of free matching money than women.

The sooner you start having the money conversation the better off you will be because the interest you can earn on money compounds over time. A great place to begin having money conversations is ensuring that you are being paid according to the market rate for your role. Then take advantage of every retirement savings vehicle your company has to offer. For example, if your organization offers a matching retirement contribution for every dollar you also contribute, contribute the maximum amount so you aren't leaving free money on the table. Second, ask for referrals for a trusted financial advisor. There are no preconditions for you to work with an advisor—you don't need to make six figures or have a savings account. There is no shame in having debt and no idea where to begin—this is what financial advisors do; they can help you set a budget based on your income and make a plan that works for you. Many advisors will offer free consultations. Also, many employers offer access to a financial advisor, so check with your benefits program to see what financial well-being assistance they offer for free.

CONVERSATION 5:
ASK FOR SUPPORT

My now retired father-in-law told me once that he learned how to be a leader from informal coaching he received from his boss at the bar after work. Several years ago, this wasn't all that uncommon. Men held the majority of leadership roles, so coaching and mentoring happened in the meeting rooms, at work check-ins, or even at the bar.

When I was in corporate, we'd promote people from employee to leader and just assumed a magic transformation would happen—that they'd shed the identity they had as a doer and transform into a leader who was comfortable coaching, delegating, and making hard decisions. As a former leader of training and leadership development programs, I admit I could have done a better job in my corporate years of recognizing the difficulty of this mindset shift and the support required to be successful at the next level. Investing in leadership development support for women is a money conversation in two ways. First, it asks for funding from her employer to ensure her development and success as a leader. Second, because men tend to receive more support after a promotion, they also tend to be more successful, which helps them sustain and grow their income. So the leadership development support that a woman receives postpromotion can also impact her confidence and success, which correlates to future salary and bonus earnings.

If you just made a career leap or earned a big promotion at work, what support can you expect to ensure your success as a leader? A DDI report, which featured input from more than fifteen thousand leaders and more than two thousand human resources directors, found men are 13 percent more likely to receive leadership skills training than women. Men are 22 percent more likely than women to be paired up with a formal mentor. Also, 22 percent more men than women participate in leadership development programs—that's nearly a quarter more of the workforce.

When it comes to leadership development opportunities, 58 percent more women than men have to ask to be included, and women reported significantly lower rates of opportunity to receive coaching from their employer. The study found that while 22 percent of men have been given access to coaching through their employer, only 16 percent of women have been offered similar opportunities.

It's time to close the leadership development gap for women, and employers can take the lead. Two ways employers can work to close the gap are in-house development and outside coaching. They can offer a standard onboarding track for newly hired leaders and promoted leaders including a mix of coaching, training, and mentoring. If employers don't have the internal resources to support an onboarding track, they can offer reimbursement. When this is the case, an effective option I've seen employers choose is to offer a stipend to newly hired leaders so they can invest their development through outside coaching or training. By offering these leaders the support they need, the benefits can include reduced turnover and improved time to effectiveness.

Women can play a part in closing the gap by proactively asking for support and investing in themselves. Whether it's inquiring about internal programs or asking for a reimbursement to cover your investment in personal leadership development resources, it pays to choose yourself—not only for your own confidence and leadership skills but also through the readiness and results you can provide the organization. Women can also create support networks or advocate for programs in their organization to help foster leadership development and mentoring needed for new leaders, especially women and minorities, who may not have benefitted from as much leadership development training.

Closing the leadership development gap isn't just the right thing to do to level the playing field for women leaders, it's a great money decision too. Research continues to show that organizations are more profitable when women are well represented at the top.

This is a decision that pays dividends for an organization's, and a woman's, paycheck.

ASK FOR WHAT YOU DESERVE

Feeling motivated by all this information but still too intimidated to ask? This is normal to feel this way, and the confidence gap research by Wharton confirms that women hesitate to self-promote, even though they know it can positively impact their career and salary. First, practice by asking for smaller wants in your life—like renegotiating your cable bill or securing a better pricing discount with a vendor at work. In his book *Give and Take*, Adam Grant writes that when we start to act on small behaviors in the direction we want, it gives us confidence and promotes a self-fulfilling prophecy and belief that we are successful at that skill. When we realize wins from negotiating the small stuff, we gain confidence to take action on the big stuff.

Second, commit to asking for everything. Beyond money, it can be hard to ask for help or what you need and want. Ask about your organization's pay philosophy. Ask your partner about your savings plans. Ask your local governments what policies they are introducing to create pay parity. Ask your organization to cover a leadership development training you've been wanting to attend. Every so often, I dedicate a week on my calendar just to ask for stuff. Yes, even though I've written many tips in this book to own your worth, amplify your voice, and overcome doubt, it doesn't mean that my own insecurities go away. For these dedicated asking days, which I often name my Ask Fest, I made a list of ten things to ask for. Some of them feel easy, like reaching out to a connection and sharing one of my business opportunities, or really far out of reach, like pitching myself to be the keynote speaker at a women's leadership conference.

I know how vulnerable it is to ask for things—I get nervous that people might think my ask is silly or they'll say no. I feel all the doubt and insecurities sending ask emails. Sometimes I just have to close my eyes, hit send, and hope for the best. But I know that by owning my worth, these asks not only help my business but have future financial benefits too. Every time I commit to an Ask Fest week, it always turns out better than I hope, and I often wonder why I procrastinated on it for so long.

Remember: talking about money isn't shameful; it's essential for women to boost their confidence for promoting themselves and closing the money gaps. As a former HR professional, I can tell you many of us in HR are ready to talk and negotiate money with candidates. Don't let us down!

Imagine what is out there waiting for you. Know your worth and make your ask.

CLOSE THE CONFIDENCE GAP
TOOL KIT

KNOW YOUR WORTH
(AND MAKE YOUR ASK)

NOTICE IT

Find the data and prep your ask.

Visit salary data resources (PayScale.com, LinkedIn, Glassdoor. com, google "state BLS Wage systems," etc.). Mark down some data points for your role and experience.

> **TIP:** Don't match your title—match your actual work. Get to know your organization's compensation philosophy or ask the hiring manager. This will help you align your ask appropriately.

- PayScale Data: _____
- LinkedIn Data: _____
- Glassdoor Data: _____
- Other Data: _____
- *What would feel like:*
  - *A good number?*
  - *A better number?*
  - *A best number?*

OWN IT

What is unique and creative about me that no one else can offer? How can these talents help others?

A unique talent I've been able to use to help my team (or company) succeed is . . .

Write your script with an example and the results.

REFRAME IT

What would I confidently ask for today if I wasn't feeling intimated, unqualified, or fearful?

List three reasons why you are qualified. List two reasons why you are worthy of the ask.

ACT ON IT

STEP ONE: PRACTICE YOUR ASK

Put it all together to prepare for your big ask! Who can help you practice this? (friend, loved one, your phone video, etc.) Write your script. Be clear and concise in your ask. *Support your ask with data, examples, stories. Show how you will help grow the organization. Most importantly, hold the belief you are qualified. Knowing and owning your worth will be revealed in your body language and perceived by others.*

STEP TWO: MAKE YOUR ASK

Sample Script for Current Role Increase

Hi, _____,

I wanted to share some information that I would like to discuss in our next one-to-one meeting.

I've been reflecting on my role/project/accomplishments and here are the top two/three ways I've _____ in the last year.

I've been doing some research around my current compensation/benefits package, and it appears there is data that supports _____ could be more in line with my current role and accomplishments.

When is my compensation coming up for review next? I'd love to talk with you about the data I've found and how my results contribute to a review.

Thank you for considering this!

Salary Negotiation Sample Script

Hi, _____,

Thank you so much for your offer of _____ and generous benefits package.

In my research, I've found the current market rate is a range of _____ – _____.

In addition, I bring the following in experience:

1. <u>Experience 1</u> that will generate <u>XYZ results</u> for you.
2. <u>Experience 2</u> that will generate <u>XYZ results</u> for you.
3. <u>Experience 3</u> that will generate <u>XYZ results</u> for you.

I believe a fair salary for the role, experience, and results is _____.
Can we discuss this a bit more?
Thank you!

Want more nonsalary ask scripts?
Visit CLOSINGTHECONFIDENCEGAP.COM/BOOKDOWNLOADS for several more scripts for your career and personal asks!

9

TAKE YOUR BRAVEST NEXT STEP

Your first step is just that: the first of many steps. For so long
I would stand still, afraid to move in any direction because I
wasn't sure which was the course I wanted to follow for the
rest of my life. Finally, someone explained to me that my
first steps did not necessarily determine one path for all
my tomorrows. There would be more decisions, and more
opportunities to make a shift should I need to do so.

ASHLEY C. FORD

F rom the time I was a teenager, I was inundated with media
messages on the best diet to follow or how to best lose
weight. Cue years of engaging the latest fad diet and exercise.
Come every holiday season, I'd eat up *all the foods* for my diet
to begin when the media told me it was best to go on said diet—
January 1. Depending on what was popular that year, cutting fat,
cutting carbs, adding protein shakes, adding fat burners, I'd be

on it. I also promised myself that this year would be the year I would go to the gym every single day before work. In addition to that, I was going to purge my pantry and cut out all junk food.

And every year for nearly a decade, I did super amazing at this diet . . . for an entire week. Then a winter Nebraska snow-storm or subzero day would hit, and my bed was *so* warm. I'd hit the snooze and sleep in for just that one day. Then one day of sleeping in and missing the gym turned into three days. Then all my coworkers who were on diets decided it was time for a Thursday-evening happy hour. I couldn't miss that, and since I'd been depriving myself for three whole weeks, I went all in on the greasy menu. Then it was Friday date night, Saturday hang-with-friends-drink-and-eat night, and I couldn't pass up my dad's spaghetti and meatballs and dessert on Sunday for family dinner.

By the last week of January, I was on my diet plan a solid three days per week. The workouts were about as frequent. By February, I decided it was all too hard to stick to a plan, and I was back in my old habits, just in time for April, when the fitness magazines told me it was time to "trim up" (I mean, trim up for *who*?) and get my bikini body (who defines a bikini body?) for summer. Cue the self-defeating process over again.

When my daughter turned four, I was finally starting to reclaim some sanity over my schedule and independence now that she was becoming more independent in her self-care, chores, and daily habits. But I felt tired, sluggish, and foggy—just bleh. My clothes didn't fit well. I lacked self-confidence in many areas of my life, not because I felt I was a few pounds over my ideal weight but because I didn't feel energetic, healthy, or strong.

One day something clicked. I didn't *feel* how I wanted to *feel*. I didn't carry the identity that I wanted for myself. I wanted to feel healthy and strong. I wanted to be in shape—not just physically in shape or even a certain scale weight—but I wanted to be in shape mentally, physically, and emotionally. I asked myself, "What would an in-shape woman do? If I was a healthy and strong woman, who would I be?" I began to visualize what it would look like to be healthy, energetic, and strong. I imagined what it would feel like to move through my day as this kind of woman. I imagined what activities I might participate in and enjoy because I had the energy for them. I closed my eyes and visualized where I could be by that time next year if I committed to embodying those feelings and identity and took action on them.

This led me quickly down a potentially dangerous path again—I began making a list of all the things I would need to do to be that—start exercising every day, follow a strict diet, get cute exercise clothes, and buy protein shakes. But then I remembered that my "dive in all at once" approach literally failed for an entire decade. So I started by writing down everything I ate that day. That's it. I'd read in one of my many fitness magazines that people who kept a food journal were successful, so I thought I'd try that.

For several weeks, that's all I did—I kept a record of what I ate. It was *very* enlightening. I learned how often I grabbed an entire handful of Hot Tamales from my coworker's jar, how large restaurant food portions truly were, and how much mindless eating I was doing—mostly because I was tired, stressed, or bored. After I had a better handle on making healthier food choices and portions, I added in walking and jogging. I did this for several more weeks. Once this became a habit, I accepted an invite to join a local kickboxing gym—it aligned perfectly with my values in this journey to feel *healthy, strong, and in shape.* And it was fun with a friend. After several months of kickboxing, I began lifting weights, which to this day is my single favorite activity to make me feel healthy and strong.

Over the course of a little over one year, I lost almost twenty pounds, but weight loss was not the goal of the mission. The goal of the journey was to feel alive, strong, healthy, and energized. I had more focus at work and less anxiety. Overall, I simply felt more awake and less tired throughout the day. I felt like a strong, energetic, and healthy woman, and overall a nicer person. Twelve years later, I'm still the same weight and have kept up my habits consistently, not because I'm killing myself trying to stick to a rigid diet or exercise routine but because I made a commitment to who I want to be, how I want to feel, and based on my values, what actions I will take to align with them. This is not a weight loss ad—I have zero advice for you to lose weight. I don't believe in diets or overexercising, because I've gone too far by getting too thin and found there's no fulfillment there, just exhaustion and body consciousness. I learned the hard way that being too thin is just as far out of alignment of feeling healthy and strong as is being out of shape. When it comes to trusting yourself and your intuition, it is counterproductive and numbs your body's desires and intuitive nudges. You are beautiful and enough as you are, and if women would own this, they could put the billion-dollar diet industry out of business overnight.

My journey to feeling healthy and strong taught me the power of having a process to reverse engineer your success based on your values and your desired identity, not through a set of harsh rules and shoulds. All my diet failures taught me that trying to make too many sweeping changes all at once is overwhelming and my psyche can't handle it—it will work hard to fight back to homeostasis. It taught me that having big goals seems easy from far away (I'm going to write a book!), but when you get to the actual steps of executing on a goal, it feels scary as hell (what the heck will I write about? I don't even know the how to structure chapters!). Claiming my desired identity and how I wanted to feel led me to question my choices: *Is this moving me closer to who I want to be and what I value?*

Most importantly, this journey changed the way I planned everything in my life—from goal setting with my teams to setting my personal goals. I simply asked: *Where do I (or we) want to be by this time next year? Who do I (we) want to be? How do I (we) want to feel?* Then I'd reverse engineer a plan to get there. As I worked the plan back from a future date to current day, I'd be left with this question: *What's my smallest, bravest next step?*

My smallest, bravest next steps have looked wildly unimpressive. In getting healthy and strong, my smallest, bravest step was to simply write down what I ate that day. In switching careers, my smallest, bravest next step was to simply write down what I know I *didn't* want to do. In leading my teams, our smallest, bravest next step often looked like drafting an email to make an ask. In leaving corporate America, my smallest, bravest next step was to just say out loud, "I am a coach." In writing this book, my smallest, bravest step was to write down *why* I wanted to write a book.

While these steps often look unimpressive on the surface, for me, they put me in motion. They shifted me out of stalling and listing my *but firsts* and into taking action.

STALLING IS EXPENSIVE

When I first started my leadership coaching business, I dug into it like any other project plan that I was launching in corporate America. I started dreaming and scheming. I opened my spreadsheet and planned out revenue, income, and expenses. When I was looking at expenses, I accounted for marketing expense, operational expense, business startup costs, and others.

But I missed a big one. I overlooked an important obstacle that is most expensive to my business (and my career!), not just in financial terms but to my future paycheck. That expense is stalling. The not doing, not acting. In the world of economics, this is opportunity cost—the cost of things we *don't do*. Why don't I act on things needed for my career or business? Most of the time, it's not because the skills are lacking, it's because my confidence is lacking. I was just plain scared of failure or looking stupid. I bought into all my doubts and *but firsts*. Stalling became the way that I avoided uncertainty. Ambiguity just felt so damn scary. I mean, what if I took action and made the wrong decision? What if I failed? What would people think?

I often used the excuse that I was holding back and waiting for clarity on the right thing to do, or that a program needed a bit more refining before I communicated it, or tweaking everything until it was "perfect." But what I was really hoping for was certainty—certainty that a future outcome would successful or that my choice would 110 percent be the right one.

I quickly realized stalling on my ideas because I feared the unknown was costing me money—when I didn't act on my ideas, I didn't make any money. My biweekly paycheck in corporate America hid this; I still got paid every other Friday. You might think that since I had the guts to call off a wedding or leap from corporate America to become an entrepreneur, I must be fearless. *Not true*. Buddhist nun Pema Chodron says, "Usually we think that brave people have no fear. The truth is that they are intimate with fear." Here are some questions I've learned to ask myself to transform my relationship with fear and determine the next right step:

1. Does this move me toward the life I want to create? Who I want to be?
2. Does this align with my values?
3. What about intuition—does this feel of peace or dread? (Remember: moving through the "right" fear won't cause harm to yourself or others.)

If the answers are *yes*, then I take my smallest, bravest next step.

SMALL STEPS CREATE BIG TRANSFORMATIONS

Social media often makes it appear that people who achieve big goals do so seemingly overnight because we don't see the small steps or changes people make behind the scenes to create transformation. According to a study from Duke University, 45 percent of our everyday actions are made up of our habits—those tiny, sometimes unconscious choices we make every day. Another shocking revelation from this study was that setting goals has less impact on our habits than we think—the small, brave choices we make every day are impacted more greatly by the cues in the environment around us and our self-identity. So someone who runs and owns the identity "I am a runner" is more likely to keep a consistent daily practice of running to achieve a goal of running a race than someone who says, "I want to run a race." Stating the goal without owning the identity beforehand doesn't provide much motivation to change the small, consistent actions needed to achieve the outcomes they desire.

Arianna Huffington, author and founder of Thrive Global and the Microsteps movement, says what many of us are likely thinking when we're ready to make a major change in our life—we imagine tackling it all at once and that our willpower will carry us through to the finale. If you're like me and you've ever tried to change too many daily routines or practices all at once, you know it's a recipe for failure. If there's one thing the ego hates most, it's uncertainty and change. Upheaving your schedule or rising to the kick-off moment of a major project is intimidating enough to make even the most courageous people feel tempted to stall, go back to the drawing board, or use perfection as an excuse not to start. Simply put, a massive change smells overwhelmingly of failure. Huffington says that science-based microsteps are new behaviors that are broken down into the smallest possible components that are "too small to fail." Practicing these microsteps builds your confidence muscles to create consistency. She also reminds us how important it is to remember the story we want to be able to tell about ourselves ("I am a healthy, energetic, and strong woman") as real change comes from the heart, not just the head.

James Clear, author of *Atomic Habits,* has a great illustration of the power of small steps—he asks us to imagine that we are flying from Los Angeles to New York City. If a pilot leaving from Los Angeles adjusts the heading just 3.5 degrees south, you will land in Washington, DC, instead of New York. Such a small change is barely noticeable at takeoff—the nose of the airplane moves just a few feet—but when the pilot's adjustment is magnified across the entire United States, you end up hundreds of miles apart. So taking a small, brave step every day may only be 1 percent better and might seem lackluster in the moment—you may not even feel like you're making progress. But when you reflect over the span of 60, 90, and especially 365 days, you'll recognize a much larger transformation has occurred. Clear says, "Success is the product of daily habits—not once-in-a-lifetime transformations."

In my own and in my clients' experiences, sometimes we stall because we are trying to take too big of a first step. If your next step scares you, first check to ensure it's aligned with your values. If it is, break it in half as many times as you need to make it feel doable, infallible.

REVERSE ENGINEER YOUR SUCCESS INTO SMALL STEPS

Michelle came through one of my women's leadership programs because she was unclear, burned out, and unhappy in her career. By the look of it on paper, she should have been on cloud nine—she worked for a Fortune 500 company with a solid reputation. She had a stable position, excellent pay and benefits, and strong relationships from her years of employment. While the company was highly regarded, it also lacked diversity—the company structure was hierarchical, rigid, and run by mostly men. Michelle wanted to find clarity on if she should stay or go. She dreamed of a role that allowed her to express more creativity in her project management work. She wanted more career advancement and the satisfaction of being continually challenged. She often wondered if it was "right" that she had to overwork herself to earn any sort of recognition. She was tired of being overlooked for title bumps and promotions. She wanted to flourish, in a place where people around her flourished and felt more in flow and creative. While all of this sounded great, she was seriously stalling because she didn't even know where to start. She was nervous that she would fail or regret her move. Just the thought of the career change process felt daunting.

So I asked her to choose a date in the future—we picked exactly one year from that date. I had her imagine, *Where do you want to be by this time next year?* We got specific; I asked her questions like:

- What time do you want to wake up? What's your morning routine?
- What time will you start work?
- What's your schedule like? What types of meetings will you have?
- What types of decisions will you make? What projects will you be working on?
- Who will you be working with? Who is helping you?
- What time will you end your day? Then what?
- What time will you go to sleep?
- How do you want to feel (three to five words)?
- What hobbies or side interests will you be enjoying?
- Who do you want to be?

Whenever I complete this practice for myself, and as Michelle also discovered, this exercise feels completely unimaginable and unattainable. It feels plain scary to see this on paper—I mean, how in the world will these even happen? However, I told Michelle the same thing I tell all my clients: you are in charge of the *what*, don't be concerned with *how* for right now. Getting obsessed with hows that are too far in the future and feeling anxious about how this will all come together is a recipe for internal system shutdown and results in stalling.

Michelle wanted to be a woman who was creative, successful, and in flow in her work. She and I worked backward to own this identity and reverse engineer her goal. I asked her what actions and small steps she would be taking, and who could be helping her in nine months so she would be on track to make her one-year outcome a reality. She mentioned she would likely be interviewing for her next role. We kept walking it back. I had her imagine what life would be like in six months. She thought she'd likely be applying for jobs and connecting on LinkedIn. In three months, she felt confident she would have a résumé and LinkedIn profile that she felt proud of and that she'd be excited to send it to future employers. She also wanted to discover and own her talents and do the work to identify what surges her energy, so that her résumé, LinkedIn, and search strategy was focused on finding a role that would align her purpose and her paycheck.

As we got closer to the present day, this is where some uncertainty kicked in, so we had to find more clarity. Her goal in the next month was to define her values and get crystal clear on if her current workplace aligned with them. This would help her make one of the first major decisions—stay or go? I asked her what she needed to accomplish in the next week, and she was stumped. "I don't even know what I want, Kelli!" So that became her task for the next week. She didn't know what she wanted, but she definitely knew what she *didn't want*. So that was her daily task—make a list of what she *didn't want* so she could see what she *did want* with a bit more clarity. It would also help her define what her values weren't. I asked her for her smallest, bravest next step. She said, "Find a place or a journal to keep a list of my 'don't wants' and 'don't values.'"

This small, brave step of simply finding a tool to keep a list of don'ts while keeping a clear focus on who she wanted to be set her next steps in motion. Michelle got clear on her don't wants, which made claiming her values much easier. She put in the effort to get clear on her unique talents, and we updated her résumé and LinkedIn—right around this same time, she was contacted by two recruiters who were searching for her skillset. She interviewed with both employers and made a final decision—trusting herself, her intuition, and which one was a better fit for who she was, what she wanted to do, and how she wanted to feel. Within seven months of having this conversation, she negotiated and accepted a salary offer for $10,000 above what she initially requested in the job application. Nothing about this process she could have predicted, but she stayed focused on the *what* and let the universe provide her with the *how*.

This feels counterintuitive because we watch other people take what seem to be huge leaps and it seems easy and effortless. But the reality is that much of our meaningful progress forward in life is the result of many small, brave steps. It comes from the courage to set healthy boundaries to protect our energy and choose supportive people and habits that will advance, not hinder, our goals. It takes consistent, small actions over time.

|| Consistency isn't sexy, but it works.

This process also works with teams. When I coach leaders who lead teams through major projects, program launches, or business transformations, we follow the exact same reverse engineering process. I used this with my own teams. We imagined where we wanted to be one year—or a specific time frame if the project had a due date—from that day and then walked it back. What did we do? Who could help us? How did we want to feel? For today's leaders, emotional intelligence is a key part of successful leadership—asking the team to consider how they want to feel brings empathy and humanity into the planning process.

SUCCESS LOVES CLARITY

My husband and I had only been dating a few months when he tagged along with me for a work trip in Scottsdale, Arizona. We decided to make a little vacation out of the opportunity, hanging out in Old Town Scottsdale. During one of our daily excursions riding Segways around town, we saw a restaurant we wanted to come back to for supper that night.

Back at the hotel, getting ready for dinner, I plugged in the name of the restaurant, Hula's Tiki, into the Uber destination field. After the driver picked us up, we started taking unusual turns and driving by scenery we didn't recognize. We just assumed the driver knew a better, faster way to get there.

I mean, there can *only be one Hula's Tiki, right*?

Wrong. I had entered Hula's Tiki into my destination field, and it defaulted to the Phoenix location, not the Scottsdale location. It was almost right—the right food, but the wrong locale. This was the beginning of one of three (yes, three) times I got directions mixed up on this trip because I lacked precision in my destination. I wasn't clear on exactly where we were headed. My husband loves to tell this story of my habit to be directionally challenged to anyone who will listen—he still married me after all of this, so it must be one of the flaws he loves.

What's my point? *Success loves clarity.*

Like I mentioned in Michelle's story, our job is to be clear on what we want, not obsessed with how it's all going to unfold, because the universe provides the how. How often are you just "kind of" clear on your goals? Be honest: Have you shared your *exact* goal with anyone? Or are you just hoping the outcome will figure itself out?

My client Beth came to work with me because she had some big career goals. She was very successful, climbing the corporate ladder in the marketing field, and she was ready to look for her first chief marketing officer position. In our initial conversation and goal setting, I asked her, "Who have you told about your goal to be a CMO?"

She laughed. "Ummm . . . *no one*, Kelli!"

When we are clear on what we want and we have the courage to tell people, the how just comes. Networks are activated. Connections go to work. Serendipity happens. Can you think of something you have in your life today that was once a goal, and looking back on how you achieved it, were there a few "coincidences" or sudden connections that made it all happen—just because you had the courage to tell someone what you wanted or to ask for help?

Clarity requires vulnerability. It's scary as hell to tell people your big goal—I mean, what if they think you're crazy? Or you put it out there and then it fails? Clarity requires confidence and courage because it's easy to hide behind ambiguity. When

I first started my business, I was initially scared to tell people. I thought maybe my not-yet-perfect website would be over-loaded with traffic and I'd be unable to handle it. If you've ever tried to launch something, you learn like I did that the opposite is often true. *The world is noisy.* People are busy. No one is paying attention to you as much as you think. I learned that my real problem wasn't exposure, it was obscurity. This is the same whether we are being clear about expressing our personal goals or communicating clearly with our teams at work. People are distracted. Inboxes are full. When we aren't clear on our goals and desires, or we don't express them, people are left to guess. Worse, they never hear about the business or project we're working on. When they don't know, they can't help, act, or choose you.

Just like using GPS, your job is to be as precise as possible, providing the right address and location of where you want to go—let the universe use the traffic and unexpected obstacles to calculate the route.

When the enduring impacts of COVID-19 hit hard in April 2020, 80 percent of my income went away nearly overnight in the form of canceled contracts and speaking engagements. I had a pity party that lasted until June, worried that I'd be forced to fold my business and rejoin the corporate ranks. Buoyed by government assistance to stay afloat, I had a decision to make about the future of my leadership coaching business. Up until that point, I offered general leadership coaching to both men and women. But my passion was for helping women and the unique challenges they experience in the workforce.

I fell back on my reverse engineering process. I imagined where my business could be one year from that day, who I would serve, and how I wanted to feel. I was tired of seeing all male decision-making rooms and wanted to attempt to make my dent in the world of it. I'd already had some success by offering my first women-only leadership program in the fall of 2019. I visualized myself moving through my day providing women's leadership training, coaching, and speaking. I felt uncertain and nervous—what if going all in on serving women would fail? What if the market wasn't there for it? What would people think? What if I shared on social media and in my client newsletters that I was focusing on women? Would that alienate corporate clients who hired me to coach their mixed-gender teams? Would I end up worse off and piss off my last prospect?

Since I'd literally lost all my income, I had nothing more to lose. So I committed to going all in on women. I made it my mission to help women advance to the rooms where decisions are made.

I reverse engineered my plan and took a small, brave next step of tweaking the following week's social media posts to talk directly to women. The response was positive. I kept consistent in my message for women, even though my confidence had ups and downs in the process. After a few months of consistent and clear messages on women, careers, and leadership, I had an aha moment. The clearer I was, the more success I realized in my new business model. As 2020 came to a close, I chose my word of the year for 2021 to be *clarity*. My mantra became *success loves clarity*, and it was plastered all over my office. I challenged myself to get even more clear on how I served women. I established consistent research time to deepen my expertise on gender-based workplace issues. This informed what I chose to advocate about and why it was important for women to consider these topics. Many of these topics are what you've read about in this book.

An even more surprising thing happened—many of the corporate clients and prospects that I thought I would lose started coming back to me and asked for my help with, you guessed it, coaching and training for their women leaders using my unique approach and philosophy. They said it became clear who I served, what I was passionate about, and the difference I would make to the women in their workplace. My business revenue nearly tripled in one year, not through hustle but from consistency and clarity.

I had no idea how my business pivot would turn out in the end. We can never be sure, but you don't have to see certainty on the outcome to take the right next step. Instead, the clarity I feared expressing turned out to create the success I was craving. Creating clarity helped me advance my life and my business with more confidence.

What would you do if you had a little more confidence? It's time to own who you are, trust yourself, and take your bravest next step.

CLOSE THE CONFIDENCE GAP TOOL KIT

TAKE YOUR BRAVEST NEXT STEPS

NOTICE IT

Where is your stalling becoming expensive for you? Where are you getting frustrated because you're trying to take too big of a first step?

OWN IT

Reflect back to your answer in the introduction of this book: If I had a little more confidence, I would _____.

What are my values and how can they guide my plan forward, even when it feels challenging?

ACT ON IT

Success loves clarity, and it's time to boost your peace, your potential, and your paycheck.

Where do you want to be by this time next year? Be specific: How do you want to feel? Who will you be with? What results will you be enjoying? Refer back to earlier sections for more question prompts here.

_____

_____

_____

Why do you want to accomplish this?

_____

_____

_____

***Who* is the type of woman who accomplishes this?**

_____

_____

_____

Word or phrase for the year that aligns to your values and talents:

_____

_____

_____

What do you need to be/do/accomplish in nine months?

_____

_____

_____

What do you need to be/do/accomplish in six months?

Write them here and get them on your calendar now!

_____

- -

- -

What do you need to be/do/accomplish in three months?

Write them here and get them on your calendar now!

_____

- -

- -

What do you need to be/do/accomplish in one month?

Write them here and get them on your calendar now!

_____

- -

- -

What do you need to be/do/accomplish in one week?

Write them here and get them on your calendar now!

_____

- -

- -

What is your smallest, bravest next step?

Write them here and get them on your calendar now!

_____

- -

- -

Visit CLOSINGTHECONFIDENCEGAP.COM/BOOKDOWNLOADS for a printable version of this tool or the entire workbook of tools in this book.

ADVANCE WITH CONFIDENCE

You wander from room to room hunting for the diamond
necklace that is already around your neck.

RUMI

ey friend,

I am so grateful that you picked up this book and have
made it to the end. Congratulations on investing in yourself
as a leader. Many concepts were covered in this book, so I
want to share with you what I often reiterate with my clients at
the end of my training or coaching sessions—the bottom lines.
If you take away nothing else from this book, I hope you leave
remembering a few things.

Ruth Bader Ginsburg was almost right when she said women
belong in all places where decisions are being made. She's right,
you belong. But it's not just enough to be in the room—women
must also be empowered to make an impact in that room.

It might be tempting to hide because of doubt or imposter syndrome. This is a normal feeling, and it doesn't need to be a career killer. It's time to stop overestimating everyone else's intelligence and underestimating your own. Trust yourself.

And here's the thing. You are already qualified to advance your career and make an impact—you don't need another degree or certification. You can be a leader and influencer while also feeling doubt (I sure do).

Everything you need to be confident and successful is *already within you*, and you'll shine when you remove what's in the way of it.

So, just for today, share your idea. Speak your voice. Lead with confidence. Own the brilliant and talented woman that you are. Trust yourself and take your bravest next step.

Remember that somebody, somewhere, is counting on your unique calling.

–Kelli

SHARE YOUR BRAVE NEXT STEPS

What did you say at the beginning of this book that you'd do if you had a little more confidence?

How can acting on this boost your peace, your potential, and your paycheck?

Write how you'll own who you are, trust yourself, or take your bravest next step. If you had a win here already, write that too.

Share these, a win, or even just an aha from this book on social media, and tag me and **#closingtheconfidencegap** so that I can support and celebrate you!

My bravest next step: _____

_____

A win I've experienced: _____

_____

My favorite book aha moment: _____

_____

ACKNOWLEDGMENTS

To my husband, Jason, this book would not exist without you in my life. Thank you for signing up for my crazy entrepreneurship journey. Thank you for listening to me read chapters out loud and proofreading endless stories. Most importantly, thank you for standing behind me and reminding me of what I'm capable of. Thank you for supporting me, my business, and Hailey—the words and stories in this book cannot do justice to how wonderful you are. You continue to amaze me with your unconditional love and support.

To Brooke, my book coach-therapist-whisperer. Thank you for reminding me to trust my intuition and bring the words inside me onto paper. Thank you for helping my book dreams become reality and providing the guidance, support, and love to keep going.

To Hailey, thank you for the wisdom you've been teaching me since you were born. You are wise and empathetic beyond your years. I am so proud to be your mom.

To my clients, this book sits on the shoulders of each and every one of you. Your stories illuminate this book. You inspire me with your goals, your bravery, and your transformations. *You* are changing the workplace and everyone in your sphere of influence.

To Cy, thank you for paving the way for me as a woman entrepreneur and showing me the power of telling stories. Because I watched you write, lead, and speak, you opened the door for me to do the same. Thank you for showing me so much support and generosity in my career and entrepreneurial journey.

To Whitney and Ellie, thank you for endless proofreads and reassurance as the book came together. Thank you for reminding me of my voice and the importance of writing this as me. Denise, Nadia, and Staci, thank you for your endless brainstorming and being a rock of consistency and support when I thought for sure that everything was falling apart. Vickie, thank you for being a such an inspiring leader and mentor for me, and now a beautiful friend.

To my parents, thank you for your love and support through all my ups and downs, especially as I messily unraveled all the "rules." You taught me first and foremost to remember who I am, and there isn't a day I don't think about that advice and work to own it. And yes, my car is still running fine, the oil is changed, and the money is holding out. Jake, I thank you every day for your unconditional support and the ability to tell me the truth in high-stakes moments. You have always given me a burst of clarity when I needed it most.

Thank you to the team at Amplify Publishing—Jess, Naren, Jenna, and Caitlin—for believing in me and my book. Your level of support and professionalism is unmatched, and I am lucky to be one of your authors.

REFERENCES

Introduction

The Confidence Gap in Work Performance Reviews Between Women and Men. (January 3, 2020).The Wharton School. https://www.wharton.upenn.edu/story/the-confidence-gap-in-work-performance-reviews-between-women-and-men/.

Women in the Workplace 2021. (2021, November 2). McKinsey & Company. https://www.mckinsey.com/featured-insights/diversity-and-inclusion/women-in-the-workplace.

Noland, M. (2016, February 8). *Study: Firms with More Women in the C-Suite Are More Profitable.* Harvard Business Review. https://hbr.org/2016/02/study-firms-with-more-women-in-the-c-suite-are-more-profitable.

Chapter 1: Claim Your Role as a Confident Leader

Beck, M. (2018, January 21). *Growing Wings: The Power of Change.* Martha Beck. https://marthabeck.com/2003/01/growing-wings-the-power-of-change/.

Brown, B. (2017). *Rising Strong: How the Ability to Reset Transforms the Way We Live, Love, Parent, and Lead* (Reprint ed.). Random House.

Mikulak, A. (2016, July 29). *The Heart of the Matter*. Association for Psychological Science—APS. https://www.psychologicalscience.org/observer/the-heart-of-the-matter.

Hayes, S. C. (2019). *A Liberated Mind: The Essential Guide to ACT*. Vermilion.

Chapter 2: Tame Your Imposter Monster

Wakeman, C., and Winget, L. (2010). *Reality-Based Leadership: Ditch the Drama, Restore Sanity to the Workplace, and Turn Excuses into Results* (1st ed.). Jossey-Bass.

Antanaityte, N. (2005). *Mind Matters: How to Effortlessly Have More Positive Thoughts*. TLEXinstitute.Com. https://tlexinstitute.com/how-to-effortlessly-have-more-positive-thoughts/.

Clance, P. R., and Imes, S. A. (1978). The Imposter Phenomenon in High Achieving Women: Dynamics and Therapeutic Intervention. *Psychotherapy: Theory, Research & Practice, 15*(3), 241–247.

McCracken, M. (2021, January 5). *The Only Thing You Need to Do to Overcome Fear, According to Neuroscience*. Inc.Com. https://www.inc.com/mareo-mccracken/this-neuroscience-trick-will-help-you-overcome-any-fear.html.

da Silva, C. (2018, December 17). *Michelle Obama Opens Up about "Imposter Syndrome."* Newsweek. https://www.newsweek.com/michelle-obama-tells-secret-i-have-been-every-powerful-table-you-can-think-1242695.

de Morree, P. (2021, November 9). *Beware: This Hippo Kills Your Company!* Corporate Rebels. https://corporate-rebels.com/hippo-effect/.

Chapter 3: It Pays to Be Yourself

Statista. (2022, January 11). *Share of Human Resources Managers in the U.S. 2020, by Gender*. https://www.statista.com/statistics/1088059/share-human-resources-managers-united-states-gender/.

Horowitz, J. M., Igielnik, R., and Parker, K. (2020, May 30). *Women and Leadership 2018*. Pew Research Center's Social and Demographic Trends Project. https://www.pewresearch.org/social-trends/2018/09/20/women-and-leadership-2018/.

Turczynski, B. (2021, July 30). *The Female Boss: How We See Women in Power [2021 Study]*. ResumeLab. https://resumelab.com/career-advice/female-boss.

Research: Women Score Higher Than Men in Most Leadership Skills. (2021, September 17). Harvard Business Review. https://hbr.org/2019/06/research-women-score-higher-than-men-in-most-leadership-skills.

Women in the Workplace 2021. (2021, November 2). McKinsey & Company. https://www.mckinsey.com/featured-insights/diversity-and-inclusion/women-in-the-workplace.

Women in the Workplace 2020. (2020). Lean In. https://leanin.org/women-in-the-workplace-report-2020#!.

Lawson, M. A., Martin, A. E., Huda, I., and Matz, S. C. (2022, February 22). Hiring Women into Senior Leadership Positions Is Associated with a Reduction in Gender Stereotypes in Organizational Language. *PNAS*, *119*(9), e2026443119. https://www.pnas.org/doi/10.1073/pnas.2026443119.

Research: It Pays to Be Yourself. (2021, September 17). Harvard Business Review. https://hbr.org/2020/02/research-it-pays-to-be-yourself.

Chapter 4: Align Your Purpose and Your Paycheck

PricewaterhouseCoopers. (2021). *PwC US Pulse Survey: Next in Work*. https://www.pwc.com/us/en/library/pulse-survey/future-of-work.html.

Goff, S. (2021, February 19). *Jill Ellis Earned More in World Cup Year but Still Not as Much as Her U.S. Men's Counterpart*. Washington Post. https://www.washingtonpost.com/sports/2021/02/19/uswnt-jill-ellis-earnings-ussf/.

Hendricks, G. (2010). *The Big Leap: Conquer Your Hidden Fear and Take Life to the Next Level* (3rd ed.). HarperOne.

Dhingra, N., Samo, A., Schaninger, B., and Schrimper, M. (2021, October 4). *Help Your Employees Find Purpose—or Watch Them Leave*. McKinsey & Company. https://www.mckinsey.com/business-functions/people-and-organizational-performance/our-insights/help-your-employees-find-purpose-or-watch-them-leave.

Manson, M. (2022, January 10). *7 Strange Questions That Help You Find Your Life Purpose*. https://markmanson.net/life-purpose.

Chapter 5: Lead More by Doing Less

Jericho, G. (2021, February 22). *Women Continue to Carry the Load When It Comes to Unpaid Work*. The Guardian. https://www.theguardian.com/business/grogonomics/2021/feb/23/women-continue-to-carry-the-load-when-it-comes-to-unpaid-work.

Wezerek, G., and Ghodsee, K. R. (2020, August 11). *Women's Unpaid Labor Is Worth $10,900,000,000,000*. The New York Times. https://www.nytimes.com/interactive/2020/03/04/opinion/women-unpaid-labor.html.

Saujani, R. (2021, May 8). *The Perfect Gift for Moms: Money*. The New York Times. https://www.nytimes.com/2021/05/07/opinion/mothers-day-gifts-money.html.

Babcock, L. (2019, November 22). *Why Women Volunteer for Tasks That Don't Lead to Promotions*. Harvard Business Review. https://hbr.org/amp/2018/07/why-women-volunteer-for-tasks-that-dont-lead-to-promotions.

Research: Women Leaders Took on Even More Invisible Work During the Pandemic. (2021, October 13). Harvard Business Review. https://hbr.org/2021/10/research-women-took-on-even-more-invisible-work-during-the-pandemic.

Chapter 6: Trust Yourself

Hatmaker, J. (Host). (31 August, 2021). Fighting Fear of Failure and Taking the Leap with Jamie Kern Lima (Series 36) [Audio podcast episode]. In *For the Love*. Jenhatmaker.Com. https://jenhatmaker.com/podcast/series-36/fighting-fear-of-failure-and-taking-the-leap-with-jamie-kern-lima/.

Beck, M. (2008). *Finding Your Own North Star*. Harmony/Rodale.

Clinical Evidence of Intuition: The Iowa Gambling Task. (2010). Science 2.0. https://www.science20.com/brain_candyfeed_your_mind/clinical_evidence_intuition_iowa_gambling_task.

Calderon, M. A. (2014, March 9). *The Bandwidth of Consciousness | Psych 256: Introduction to Cognitive Psychology*. Penn State University. https://sites.psu.edu/psych256sp14/2014/03/09/the-bandwidth-of-consciousness/.

Soosalu, G., Henwood, S., and Deo, A. (2019). Head, Heart, and Gut in Decision Making: Development of a Multiple Brain Preference Questionnaire. *SAGE Open*, *9*(1), 215824401983743. https://doi.org/10.1177/2158244019837439.

Chapter 7: Amplify Your Voice and Make an Impact

Catalyst. (2021, March 3). *Campaign Provides Virtual Meeting Backgrounds to Call Out Bias in the Workplace.* https://www.catalyst.org/media-release/bias-correct-iwd-2021/.

Tulshyan, R. (2021, March 16). *Why Is It so Hard to Speak Up at Work?* The New York Times. https://www.nytimes.com/2021/03/15/us/workplace-psychological-safety.html.

University of Maryland's Robert H. Smith School of Business. (2021, March 31). *When Women Managers Speak Up, Others Will Follow: New Study*. https://www.prnewswire.com/news-releases/when-women-managers-speak-up-others-will-follow-new-study-301259413.html.

Beck, M. (2021, June 16). *How Many People Have Infertility?* RESOLVE: The National Infertility Association. https://resolve.org/how-many-people-have-infertility/.

Black, R. (2019, September 12). *Glossophobia (Fear of Public Speaking): Are You Glossophobic?* Psycom. https://www.psycom.net/glossophobia-fear-of-public-speaking.

Arnold, C. (2021, May 3). *How Do Sea Turtles Find the Exact Beach Where They Were Born?* National Geographic. https://www.nationalgeographic.com/animals/article/150115-loggerheads-sea-turtles-navigation-magnetic-field-science.

Chapter 8: Know Your Worth

U.S. Census Bureau. (2021, October 15). *Women Represent Majority of Workers in Several Essential Occupations*. https://www.census.gov/library/stories/2021/03/unequally-essential-women-and-gender-pay-gap-during-covid-19.html.

Dickler, J. (2019, April 2). *Equal Pay Day Highlights a $1 Million Salary Shortfall for Some Women*. CNBC. https://www.cnbc.com/2019/04/02/the-gender-pay-gap-can-add-up-to-a-1-million-shortfall.html.

Stieg, C. (2020, March 31). *How the Gender Pay Gap Affects Women's Mental Health*. CNBC. https://www.cnbc.com/2020/03/31/how-the-gender-pay-gap-affects-womens-mental-health.html.

U.S. Bank Survey Says Women Are Leaving Money and Influence on the Table. (2021, April 22). Company Blog, U.S. Bank. https://www.usbank.com/about-us-bank/company-blog/article-library/us-bank-survey-says-women-are-leaving-money-and-influence-on-the-table.html.

Sun, S. (2021, January). *Policy Brief. On the Books, Off the Record: Examining the Effectiveness of Pay Secrecy Laws in the U.S.* Institute for Women's Policy Research. https://iwpr.org/wp-content/uploads/2021/01/Pay-Secrecy-Policy-Brief-v4.pdf.

WorldatWork. (2020, March 5). *Workspan Magazine—Workspan by WorldatWork*. https://worldatwork.org/workspan/articles/how-pay-transparency-benefits-businesses.

Tockey, D., and Ignatova, M. (2018). *Gender Insights Report: How Women Find Jobs Differently*. LinkedIn. https://business.linkedin.com/content/dam/me/business/en-us/talent-solutions-lodestone/body/pdf/Gender-Insights-Report.pdf.

Nice Girls Don't Ask. (2014, August 1). Harvard Business Review. https://hbr.org/2003/10/nice-girls-dont-ask.

Callahan, A. (2020, October 22). *Why Women Make Great Investors*. Wells Fargo Stories. https://stories.wf.com/women-make-great-investors/.

Rosato, D. (2015, June 9). *Women Are Better Retirement Savers Than Men, but Still Have a Lot Less*. Money. https://money.com/retirement-401ks-women-men/.

Defining the Gender Gap in Coaching: What It Is and How to Fix It. (2021, April 6). BetterUp. https://www.betterup.com/blog/coaching-gender-gap#:%7E:text=We%20found%20that%20while%2022,a%20disproportionate%20access%20to%20it.

Smedley, M. (2021, June 21). *Gender Bias: A Problem from Day One*. DDI. https://ddiworld.medium.com/gender-bias-a-problem-from-day-one-dbe0a9aeb0c7.

Grant, A. (2014). *Give and Take: Why Helping Others Drives Our Success* (Reprint ed.). Penguin Books.

Chapter 9: Take Your Bravest Next Step

Neal, D. T., Wood, W., and Quinn, J. M. (2006). *Habits—A Repeat Performance*. USC.Edu. https://dornsife.usc.edu/assets/sites/545/docs/Wendy_Wood_Research_Articles/Habits/Neal.Wood.Quinn.2006_Habits_a_repeat_performance.pdf.

Huffington, A. (2019, February). *Microsteps: The Big Idea That's Too Small to Fail*. Thrive Global. https://thriveglobal.com/stories/microsteps-big-idea-too-small-to-fail-healthy-habits-willpower/.

Clear, J. (2019). *Atomic Habits: An Easy and Proven Way to Build Good Habits and Break Bad Ones* (1st ed.). Penguin Random House USA.

ABOUT THE AUTHOR

Kelli Thompson is a women's leadership coach and speaker who helps women advance to the rooms where decisions are made. She has coached and trained hundreds of women to trust themselves, lead with more confidence, and create a career they love. She is the founder of the Clarity & Confidence Women's Leadership Program, and a Stevie Award® winner for Women in Business—Coach of the Year.

Kelli holds an MBA, has served as an adjunct management professor, and has more than ten years of senior leadership experience in financial services and technology organizations. Her thought leadership has been featured in *Forbes*, *MarketWatch*, *Parents Magazine*, *HuffPost*, and *Working Mother*. Kelli is from Omaha, Nebraska, and her favorite roles are wife to Jason and mom to Hailey.